MALLARD

and the A4 Class

MALLARD

and the A4 Class

David McIntosh

Ian Allan
PUBLISHING

First published 2008

ISBN 978 0 7110 3297 2

© Ian Allan Publishing 2008

Published by Ian Allan Publishing

an imprint of Ian Allan Publishing Ltd,
Hersham, Surrey KT12 4RG
Printed in England by Ian Allan Printing Ltd
Hersham, Surrey KT12 4RG

Code: 0806/D2

Visit the Ian Allan Publishing website at
www.ianallanpublishing.com

Title Page
On 14th April 1979 No 4498 *Sir Nigel Gresley* climbs up the 1in182 grade out of the Wharfe valley towards Weeton station with a clockwise 'York Circular' excursion. The stainless steel letters and numbers carried by No 4498 were re-instated prior to the 'S&D 150' event at Shildon in 1975.
Mel Haigh/A4 LS

CONTENTS

Bibliography

Peter Coster	The Book of the A4 Pacifics	Irwell Press 2005
Michael Harris	LNER Carriages	Atlantic Publishers 1995
Geoffrey Hughes	The Gresley Influence	Ian Allan 1983
Geoffrey Hughes	LNER	Ian Allan 1996
Geoffrey Hughes	Sir Nigel Gresley, the engineer and his family	Oakwood 2001
Roger Mannion	The Streaks, Gresley's A4s.	Sutton Publishing 1997
O.S.Nock	The Gresley Pacifics	David & Charles 1982
RCTS	Locomotives of the LNER. 2A Tender Engines A1 to A10	RCTS 1973
Michael Rutherford	Mallard, the Record Breaker	NRM 1988/2004
Bill Sharman	Main Line Steam	Atlantic Publishers 1997
P.N.Townend	Top Shed	Ian Allan 1975
P.N.Townend	East Coast Pacifics at Work	Ian Allan 1982
W.B.Yeadon	Register of LNER Locomotives Vol 2 A4 & W1	Irwell Press 2001

INTRODUCTION

My first encounter with an 'A4' is still clear in my memory and came in 1957. As part of a locospotting trip from my home in North Wales to Doncaster over a route now largely abandoned, I had travelled from Shotton High Level station via Chester Northgate and Northwich to Manchester Central behind ex-GC 'C14' and 'D11' types, before joining the daily Liverpool Central to Hull express for the journey via Woodhead to Doncaster. From Manchester Central to Guide Bridge I was hauled by a Fowler 2-6-4 tank before an EM2 Co-Co electric whisked me over the Pennines to Sheffield Victoria. The last leg of my trip was hauled by a 'K3' and, soon after my arrival in Doncaster, from the assembled throng of spotters arose the unfamiliar (to me, at least) cry of 'Streak!' This was quickly followed by a long chime whistle burst of an unforgettable tone as the 'A4' heading the northbound 'Flying Scotsman' roared through on the down fast line. Subsequent visits to Leeds Central and York imprinted on my memory the tingle of sheer ecstasy that an 'A4' chime whistle still generates to this day.

In 1962 I began a long association with the Ffestiniog Railway when I commenced training as a fireman. My principal instructor was none other than ex-King's Cross top link driver Bill Hoole, who had for many years prior to his retirement in 1959 been the regular driver of 'A4' No 60007 *Sir Nigel Gresley*. I shared footplates with Bill for many thousands of miles and I like to think that I owe much of my current enginemanship skills to his kindness and endless patience with an enthusiastic schoolboy. Bill became my mentor and our friendship continued until his untimely death some years past his second retirement from the footplate. I still make occasional visits to his grave and that of his wife Dolly alongside the Ffestiniog Railway at Minffordd.

My next close association with an 'A4' came in 1980 when, as BR Area Manager Northwich, I was asked by David Ward if I could provide a temporary home in the still extant steam locomotive shed at Northwich for several locomotives before and after the 'Rocket 150' celebrations at Rainhill. Thus one morning there was a knock on my door that provided my introduction to the then custodian of 'A4' No 4498 *Sir Nigel Gresley*, Julian Riddick. Julian and I became firm friends and he introduced me to the organisation then known as the SLOA, now the Mainline Steam Locomotive Operators Association, for which I have served as Operations Director since 1995. I subsequently became a life member of the Sir Nigel Gresley Locomotive Preservation Trust, and a Trustee in 2005.

A connection with the 'A4s' of which I have only recently become aware came while researching for this book; I noted that when Nigel Gresley was nominated for membership of the Institution of Locomotive Engineers his proposer was none other than my distant relative John Farquarson McIntosh, formerly Locomotive, Carriage & Wagon Superintendent of the Caledonian Railway!

CHAPTER ONE

THE ERA OF HIGH-SPEED RAIL IN ENGLAND

When, on 14 November 2007, the new 68-mile-long 'HS1' high-speed line opened between St Pancras and the Channel Tunnel, it was only the latest development in fast passenger rail transport in England, an era that had begun on 30 September 1935. On that date at 10.00am at Newcastle Central station, locomotive No 2509 *Silver Link* departed for King's Cross with the 'Silver Jubilee' train and the new era in high-speed rail transport that ultimately led to the InterCity 125 and Eurostar had begun. The explanation of how that train was designed and built in only five months forms the first part of our story. To begin we can use no better source than the Address to the Institution of Mechanical Engineers by its President, and the designer of both locomotive and train, Sir Nigel Gresley, given on 23 October 1936:

'I visited Germany in the latter part of 1934 and travelled on the "Flying Hamburger" from Berlin to Hamburg and back; I was so much impressed by the smooth running of this train at a speed of 100mph, which was maintained for long distances, that I thought it advisable to explore the possibilities of extra-high-speed travel by having such a train for experimental purposes on the London & North Eastern Railway.

'I accordingly approached the makers of that train and furnished them with full particulars as to the gradients, curves and speed restrictions on the line between King's Cross and Newcastle. With the thoroughness characteristic of the German engineers they made a very exhaustive investigation and prepared a complete schedule showing the shortest possible running times under favourable conditions and then added 10%

which they regarded as adequate to meet varying weather conditions and to have sufficient time in reserve to make up for such decelerations or delays as might normally be expected.

'The train, weighing 115 tons, was to consist of three articulated coaches and to be generally similar to the German train. The times for the complete journey were given as 4 hours 15½ minutes in the down direction. The train provided seating for 140 passengers. The accommodation was much more cramped than that provided in this country for ordinary 3rd Class passengers, and it did not appear likely to prove attractive for a journey occupying four hours. My Chief General Manager (Sir Ralph Wedgwood) suggested that with an ordinary "Pacific" engine faster overall speeds could be maintained with a train of much greater weight, capacity, and comfort. A trial with a train of seven bogie coaches demonstrated that the run could be accomplished with reliability in less than 4 hours under normal conditions.

'I felt that to secure a sufficient margin of power it would be essential to streamline the engine and train as effectively as possible, and at the same time to make sundry alterations to the design of cylinders and boiler which would conduce to freer running and to securing an ample reserve of power for fast uphill running. The designs for the engine and carriages were prepared and the complete train built in the company's works at Doncaster in the remarkably short time of five months, and I am pleased to place on record this achievement of my staff.

'The train was completed early in September of last year and after a few runs on which exceptionally high speeds were reached, went into service on 30th September. It completed twelve months' service of five days weekly on 30th September last, and had run 133,464 miles during that period and carried about 68,000 passengers. There has only once been an engine failure when the train had to be stopped and another engine substituted.'

Displaying the modesty with which he was typically associated, Gresley acknowledged the contribution of Ralph Wedgwood to the decision to opt for a steam-hauled solution to the problem. Indeed, Gresley was fortunate that the LNER, unlike its larger LMS rival, enjoyed a long period of stability in the senior management team, which led to the ability to make rapid decisions and firm implementations typified

by the 'Silver Jubilee' project. The Chairman, William Whitelaw, Chief General Manager (Chief Executive in modern parlance), Ralph Wedgwood, and Chief Mechanical Engineer, Nigel Gresley, had all been in post and therefore working closely together for 11 years since the formation of the LNER in 1923. They all knew and trusted each other intimately through many years of close collaboration and this gave the LNER a firmness of purpose that held it in good stead through the often difficult times of the 1930s. Wedgwood often displayed a strong commercial flair, which manifested itself in a number of strikingly successful initiatives, of which the ultimate trio of high-speed passenger services was but one example.

No 2509 *Silver Link* coasts over Langley water troughs in preparation for the 1 in 200 climb towards Knebworth on the southbound seven-coach 'Silver Jubilee' in August 1937. The engine had recently received extended front buffers, but was not to acquire a cast nameplate until the following December. The 'Silver Jubilee' gained an eighth coach in February 1938. *Real Photographs* T5446

CHAPTER TWO

THE GENESIS OF THE 'A4' PACIFIC

The 'A1' Pacifics

In April 1922 the first of Gresley's Pacifics, No 1470 *Great Northern*, emerged from Doncaster Works. This new design of locomotive incorporated all three of the distinctive design principles with which Gresley was to become associated throughout his career. One was the use of three-cylinder propulsion with the operation of the inside valves derived from the valve gear of the outside cylinders. Initially Gresley had rebuilt an Ivatt Atlantic in 1915 with four cylinders and outside Walschaerts valve gear operating the inside piston valves by means of rocking shafts, but in 1916 his attention had been drawn to the publication in *Engineering* of detailed drawings of a Pennsylvania

Railroad 'K4s' Pacific, and he is reported to have been very impressed by the locomotive's proportions. The GNR structure gauge could not accommodate the large outside cylinders of the two-cylinder 'K4s', and the three-cylinder arrangement had already been successfully applied by Gresley in 1918 to a version of his 2-8-0, and in 1920 to the enlarged 2-6-0 that became the 'K3'. Gresley therefore settled on the three-cylinder arrangement as offering the advantages of a more even turning moment leading to less wear and tear to a locomotive's motion and a significant reduction in the 'hammer blow' experienced with two-cylinder designs; this in turn offered less wear on the track and structures and the possibility of lighter valve gear and reciprocating parts.

The original Gresley Pacific, No 1470 *Great Northern*, was delivered by Doncaster in March 1922. She was only the second GNR locomotive to be honoured with a name, the other being the first Ivatt Atlantic, No 990 *Henry Oakley*, now preserved. Note how neat and well-proportioned the locomotive appears, contrasting greatly with its awkward and ungainly proportions when rebuilt in 1944 by Thompson. The locomotive (actually thought to be No 1471 suitably disguised) was photographed on 23 May 1922 to show the top leading corner of the tender side already cut back. *Kingsway/KRM 075904*

The other two principles were that all three cylinders should drive on to the same axle, and that this should not be the leading coupled axle.

Great Northern was, of course, not Britain's first Pacific, that honour belonging to Churchward's *The Great Bear* of 1908 for the Great Western Railway. But whereas the GWR Pacific could hardly be regarded as a successful design, and remained the sole representative of its class, Gresley had produced a design that, with later modifications, was to extend to a total of 114 engines. He incorporated all that he considered best in contemporary British and US practice – a large boiler with a wide firebox, three cylinders and a high running plate – all contributing to a well-proportioned Pacific. The original 'A1' Pacific had a front-end designed on lines that at that date were more or less traditional in Great Britain. The valve motion was arranged with a maximum travel of 4⁹⁄₁₆ inches at 75% cut-off. This was the biggest cut-off at which the engines could be worked, the limitation being due to the fact that, in the previous 'K3' 2-6-0s, the covers of their inside cylinder valve chests were being damaged by the overrunning of the valve spindle when coasting at their full 75% cut-off with the regulator shut. With such a valve setting the 'A1s' had therefore to be worked at long cut-offs, often up to 45 or 50% with the fastest and heaviest trains, and with partially closed regulators. Their well-designed boilers and the sharp blast resulting from such methods of working always guaranteed plenty of steam, but at a cost of an average coal consumption on all duties, heavy and light, as high as 50lb per mile. However, Gresley's objective for the class was the ability to haul 600-ton trains to the schedules of the day, with average speeds of around 50mph, and this they proved well capable of doing.

The 1925 Locomotive Exchanges

The LNER was rightly proud of its new Pacifics, and in 1924 arranged for the third engine, and the first post-Grouping example, No 4472 *Flying Scotsman*, to appear as an exhibit in the Palace of Engineering at the British Empire Exhibition at Wembley. Next to No 4472 was the newly completed GWR 4-6-0 No 4073 *Caerphilly Castle*. Noticeably smaller and of an earlier, Edwardian, appearance, the 'Castle' carried a prominent notice proclaiming it to be the most powerful locomotive in the British Isles. As it was of modest size in comparison with the 'A1', this became a talking point. The

At the end of April 1925, just before the commencement of the exchange trials, the East Coast rivals are posed at King's Cross shed. To the left is No 4079 *Pendennis Castle* and to the right unmodified standard Pacific No 4475 *Flying Fox. F. Moore/ KRM 075914*

matter was to be settled by trial when in 1925 exchanges were arranged whereby the LNER Pacific was to run on the Great Western in comparative tests with a native 'Castle', while the Pacific and a 'Castle' would be similarly pitted against one another on the LNER. Surprisingly, Gresley was apparently not consulted before the trials were instituted; they were said to have been the result of a social conversation between Sir Felix Pole, the GWR General Manager, and, depending on the source, either Ralph Wedgwood or Alex Wilson, the LNER Southern Area Divisional General Manager.

Gresley agreed with his opposite number, Collett of the GWR, that the results would not be publicised until both had had the opportunity to analyse them properly. Paddington, however, had other ideas and made much of the claimed 'victory' of its locomotives. Indeed, the 'Castles', with Churchward's valve setting and 225lb pressure, had proved that they could make better times than the 180lb-pressure Gresley engines, and with a lower fuel consumption, whether with Welsh or Yorkshire coal. O. S. Nock relates the story that Gresley visited Paddington early in the week of the trials with the 'Cornish Riviera Express' to meet No 4474 (then unnamed but later *Victor Wild*) and her crew on arrival.

The LNER footplate representative was E. D. Trask, later to become Locomotive Running Superintendent for the Southern Area of the LNER. Answering a query as to how they were doing, Trask is reported to have replied, 'All right, but not as well as the GW.' Gresley is supposed to have responded, 'Oh, but you must,' to which Trask replied, 'I don't see how we can. They've got a better valve gear than ours.' Gresley apparently retorted, 'Mr Wintour [Locomotive Works Manager at Doncaster] is getting out a modified form of ours,' to which Trask replied, 'Well, that won't be much good to us this week!'

On the LNER the tests were conducted between London and Grantham or Doncaster, the locomotives involved being GWR No 4079 *Pendennis Castle* and No 4475 *Flying Fox'*. On her very first down trip No 4475 failed with a hot box and had to be replaced by No 2545 *Diamond Jubilee*. The result was not all bad for the LNER as Gresley was forced to reconsider elements of his Pacific design, particularly the poor valve events given by the short-travel valve gear, so that ultimately the losers came to benefit most from the experience.

The 'A3' Pacifics

Bert Spencer, Gresley's chief technical assistant and the man responsible for the design of the characteristic 'Gresley' cab, had already tried in 1924 to persuade his boss to introduce long-lap, long-travel valve gear without success. Not afraid of a little industrial espionage, the LNER had had the valve gear arrangements of No 4079 *Pendennis Castle* examined at Doncaster shed before the trials in April 1925, and in June of the same year No 4082 *Windsor Castle*, while stabled in Faverdale Wagon Works prior to exhibition at the Stockton & Darlington Railway centenary celebrations, was similarly examined. The CME's reluctance to alter a design that was still comparatively new and which, although with some concerns regarding fuel consumption, was master of the tasks it was being

The first 'A1' Pacific to have the new standard arrangement of long-travel valves (note the casing above the running plate, outboard of the outside steam pipe) was No 2555 *Centenary*. Originally delivered from Doncaster in 1924, No 2555 was in the works for repairs in December 1926 and was selected by Spencer for the full modifications, emerging at the end of March 1927. A footplate trip by Gresley convinced him that the significant fuel economy demonstrated was worth replicating and the instruction to modify all of the Pacifics followed in May. In this photo from April 1927 No 2555 stands on King's Cross Top Shed. *F. Moore/KRM 075926*

set, was understandable. Eventually in 1926 Spencer was allowed to fit his own design of valve gear, first to 'A1' No 4477 *Gay Crusader*, with 1½-inch instead of 1¼-inch lap, then to 'A1' No 2555 *Centenary*, which also had its maximum valve travel increased to 5¾ inches. New narrow-ringed piston valves were also fitted and the locomotive was tested on the road where it showed remarkable fuel economy, average fuel consumption falling to 38lb per mile from the original 50lb.

After Gresley took the opportunity to observe this more economical working personally from the footplate, he ordered all of the class to be so altered. He had also been convinced that the higher boiler pressure of the GWR engines had something to do with their economy, so in 1927 a higher-pressure 220lbs/sq in boiler, which also had a much larger superheater, was fitted to Nos 4480 *Enterprise* and 2544 *Lemberg*. The locomotives were an instant success and extremely powerful, so much so that future 'A3s' (for this was the prototype) were built with smaller 19 x 26-inch cylinders. From August 1928 to February 1935 Doncaster turned out 27 new 'A3s' and all but the first

of the 'A1s' were rebuilt to conform. All valve gear modifications were completed by 1931, but the higher-pressure boiler conversions took much longer, only being completed during the war years. The typical LNER sense of economy dictated that new boilers would only be constructed when the useful life of the originals had expired.

The non-stop 'Flying Scotsman'

The economy of the new engines now facilitated a change in train working that saw, in the summer timetable of 1928, the principal daytime Anglo-Scottish express, the 'Flying Scotsman', altered to commence the longest non-stop schedule in railway history, the 392-mile journey from King's Cross to Edinburgh. In part this was a response to the initiative of the LMS, which had, with the winter 1927/8 timetable, begun to run the newly named 'Royal Scot' non-stop over the 299 miles between Euston and Carlisle. The winter portion of this train included a six-coach portion with its own dining and kitchen car for Edinburgh, so this was in direct competition with the LNER service from King's

No 4487 *Sea Eagle* puts on a fine display as she heads the 12-coach summer non-stop northbound 'Flying Scotsman' past Burnmouth in 1939. No 4487 was the first 'A4' to be 'unfrocked' in 1941 and became *Walter K. Whigham* in 1947 before becoming No 60028 in 1948.
E. R. Wethersett/IAL

Cross. The old 'gentleman's agreement' on minimum times to Edinburgh still applied, but the publicity value of the 'non-stop' claim could not be ignored.

However, it had been felt that the limit of the powers of a single engine crew had been reached in the Newcastle non-stop of the previous year and that it was undesirable on grounds of safety to carry two crews on one engine, so the idea of the corridor tender was conceived. In addition to the corridor feature, the tender was redesigned to carry an extra ton of coal. Thus at 10.00am on 1 May 1928 the longest non-stop working in the world ever to be worked by a locomotive of any kind was inaugurated by No 4472 *Flying Scotsman* from King's Cross and No 2580 *Shotover* from Edinburgh Waverley. The publicity to be derived from this service was so important that on 27 April, five days before the new service began operation, the LMS split the 'Royal Scot' into two portions and both ran non-stop over the 401 miles to Glasgow and the 399 miles to Edinburgh. This exercise was clearly designed solely to steal the LNER's thunder and was not repeated.

It is worth noting that during the summer of 1935 the Pacifics used on the non-stop 'Flying Scotsman' covered a total of 47,000 miles with a loss of only three minutes booked against the locomotive. Only two late arrivals were noted, both due to permanent way slacks.

The 'Flying Hamburger' and the test runs of 1934/5

As we have seen from his Presidential address, Gresley had taken a keen interest in the high-speed 'Flying Hamburger' diesel train, reporting on its performance to the LNER Board in the spring of 1934; then, in September of that year, he actually led a party visit to Germany in order to ride on the train. A decision of the LNER Board on 29 June to pursue further investigations led to details of the King's Cross to Newcastle route being supplied to the train's manufacturer, Maybach Motorenbau, with a view to an experimental service for the LNER. The results of this evaluation were disappointing, as the best overall journey times on offer were 4hr 15min in the down direction and 4hr 17min in the up direction.

The average speed of only 62.5mph compared with the 77.8mph achieved in Germany reflected the much more demanding nature of the East Coast route, with heavy gradients and severe speed restrictions not found between Berlin and Hamburg. Equally the diesel unit's spartan passenger accommodation for only 140 3rd Class passengers, and offering only a cold buffet for refreshment, was felt to be unacceptable.

Encouraged by Wedgwood, Gresley set out to demonstrate what could be achieved by his latest Pacifics. First, on Friday 30 November 1934, a high-speed test run was arranged between King's Cross and Leeds. Surprisingly, modified 'A1' Pacific No 4472 *Flying Scotsman* was chosen for the train, rather than one of the new 'A3' engines. It is possible that it was the choice of driver that dictated the use of No 4472, as it was the regular engine of Bill Sparshatt, who had recently been making a name for himself as a hard runner on the Pullman trains and had come to the attention of the Southern Division Locomotive Running Superintendent, I. S. W. Groom, who apparently made the selection of engine and crew for the special. Gresley held thinly disguised ambitions to make the LNER pre-eminent in locomotive speed and performance, and the return run from Leeds would give the opportunity to try for a record down Stoke bank. It was known that once the idea had been mooted, Sparshatt would need little encouragement to rise to the challenge!

To mirror the accommodation offered by its German diesel competitor the special was only loaded to four carriages on the outward down journey. The outstanding achievements were an average speed of 90.2mph over the 24.1 miles from Hitchin to Offord, with a maximum of 94.75mph, an average speed of 82.2mph over the ascent from Helpston to Stoke, and a journey time to Leeds of 2hr 31min, a record that was destined to stand for more than 30 years until well into the diesel era. For the return up journey two more coaches were attached to the train, but an overall time of 2hr 37min was still a great achievement. A world first was claimed, for a fully authenticated maximum speed of 100mph was recorded in the dynamometer car at the location between Little Bytham and Essendine to become more famous less than four years later. The whole round trip was made at an average speed of 72.2mph. Credit should also be paid to Bill Sparshatt's regular mate, fireman Webster. That a British steam train could equal its German diesel rival had been conclusively demonstrated.

On 4 January 1935 Wedgwood presented a paper to the LNER Board summarising the investigations to date, the results of the high-speed test of the previous November and the scope for further service accelerations. His proposals were approved and the scene was set for the second test run on 5 March 1935, a much harder task than that previously set for Sparshatt and No 4772. This time Class A3 Pacific No 2750 *Papyrus* was to be given the job of hauling six coaches from King's Cross to Newcastle and back on a 4-hour schedule in both directions. The outward journey, worked by Driver Gutteridge, was completed 3 minutes inside schedule in a net time of only 3hr 50min, despite a severe delay due to a freight train derailment at Shaftholme. Driver Sparshatt was in charge on the return journey, and he managed to wind up No 2750 to a new world record maximum speed of 108mph. In fact, no fewer than four new world records were established: 12.3 miles at 100.6mph average speed; 500 miles at 72.7mph average speed by one locomotive in one day with a 217-ton train; 300miles of one round trip at an average speed of 80mph; and the new maximum of 108mph. The return journey time was just under 3hr 52 min gross, 3hr 48min net.

From the viewpoint of the future policy of the LNER the day's running had been an immense success, and three days later, at the Company AGM on 8 March, Wedgwood announced the proposed new high-speed service, to be called the 'Silver Jubilee'. Three weeks later, on 28 March, his paper to the Traffic Committee was accepted and authority was given for the commencement of the design and construction of the new high-speed train and locomotives, which, as already mentioned, emerged only five months later as the 'Silver Jubilee'. Four more 'A3' Pacifics had been included in the locomotive building programme for 1935, and this gave Gresley the opportunity to anticipate the motive power requirements for regular high-speed operations by modifying the design of the 'A3' in several important areas, and thus was born the 'A4'.

Important dimensional changes in the new 'A4' Pacifics included a boiler shortened by a foot, compensated for by a corresponding lengthening of the combustion chamber, and an increase in boiler pressure to 250lb/sq in; the cylinders were 18.5 x 26 inches and the tractive effort was 35,455lb. The diameter of the valves was increased to 9 inches and special attention was paid to the internal streamlining of the steam passages, in order to ease the flow of steam into and away from the cylinders. The main steam pipe cross-sectional area was increased by 96% and the branch pipes from the superheater header by 24%. One significant impact of these changes was that, when working hard with full regulator, the steam chest pressure was almost equal to the boiler pressure, a clear indication of a highly efficient front end. Gresley had considered the use of the Kylchap blastpipe used on the 'P2' class 2-8-2s, but instead decided to use a single example with a jumper top as used by the GWR. One consideration must have been that the Kylchap exhaust system would have required the payment of royalties, which would have amounted to 5% of the overall cost of the 'A4'. In fact, Gresley reportedly confirmed not long before his death that all 'A4s' were to be so fitted when the patent expired!

The first four 'A4s' were attached to new corridor tenders of similar design to the 'A3' type introduced in 1928 for the non-stop 'Flying Scotsman' service. With the second 1936 batch of 'A4s', Nos 4482-4490 were provided with rebuilt corridor tenders, transferred from 'A1s' and 'A3s', which received new tenders or spare GN ones. Then Nos 4491-4497 had new corridor tenders built and No 4498 received the tender from *Papyrus*, which had become available after the last 'A3' run on the non-stop. The 22nd corridor tender remained with the 'W1' until June 1948, when tenders were swapped with No 4462 (by then No 60004).

The 'P2' Mikados

Before moving on to the 'A4' locomotives, in 1934 Gresley had brought out for the specialised requirements of the Edinburgh to Aberdeen line two spectacular 2-8-2 locomotives. These incorporated many innovative design features, several of which came to be replicated in the 'A4' class. Gresley had maintained a regular correspondence with his opposite numbers in France and had taken careful note of the ability of the Nord Pacifics of M Collin to lift a 600-ton train up the 1 in 125 gradient of the Caffiers bank soon after a 'cold' start from Calais, and of the Chapelon Pacifics of the Paris-Orleans to regularly run 800-ton trains at the French maximum speed of 74mph on level track.

The 'P2s' therefore incorporated a Kylchap (Kylala/Chapelon) double blastpipe and had the inside steam passages thoroughly streamlined. They also incorporated the wedge-shaped cab front that was a feature of current French practice. All were features to be carried forward into the design of the 'A4', although the Kylchap exhaust only appeared in March 1938 on the 28th locomotive, No 4468 *Mallard*, then on the final three locomotives in June and July 1938.

External streamlining

Both the 'P2s' of 1934, and the solitary experimental high-pressure 'W1' of 1929, also had experimented with limited external streamlining. Although energy-saving, and thus fuel-saving, was the initial motivation, secondary to this was dealing with the problem common to large-boilered locomotives designed to be worked at short cut-offs, namely drifting smoke obscuring the driver's view of signals and the line ahead. Initially Gresley was a sceptic regarding the benefits to be obtained by external streamlining, but when calculations demonstrated that at above 75mph the reductions possible in air resistance offered the real advantage of power savings of up to 40%, he gave authority for his assistant, Oliver Bulleid, to develop the detailed designs Gresley himself commented on at the Institution of Railway Engineers in the autumn of 1934, that 'experiments with models of existing types of coaches carried out by NPL [the National Physical Laboratory] show that air resistance of trains of average length, say, 12 coaches, at 100mph is approximately double that of similar trains at 70mph... Streamlining is essential at extra high speed because the air resistance increases approximately with the square of the speed.'

Gresley had noted the wedge-shaped front end of the Bugatti high-speed railcar on which he had travelled between Paris and Deauville, and this shape was incorporated in a series of wind tunnel tests undertaken on models at both the NPL and the City & Guilds Institute. Initially the top of the boiler casing behind the chimney was flat. However, prior to one test an unknown finger made an indentation in the plasticine mould immediately behind the chimney and Professor Dalby, of the C&GI, noted that this 'accidental modification' gave much improved smoke-lifting. Indeed, this highly distinctive feature of the 'A4' is probably the most successful example of effective design in its ability to lift smoke clear of the boiler side at even moderate speeds.

The wedge-shaped front end of the 'A4s' meant that the smokebox door could not be completely circular in shape. The streamlined casing at the very front of the smokebox consisted of two large hinged doors, by which means access was facilitated to the smokebox door and the smokebox itself. These doors were opened by mechanical gearing actuated by a detachable handcrank, so positioned that it could be used by a man standing at ground level. This method of opening the 'cod's mouth' apparently had its origin in a Doncaster plant draughtsman observing the operation of the rear door mechanism of a Doncaster Corporation dustcart!

The first 'A4', No 2509 *Silver Link*, gets an admiring going-over by staff after arrival at Top Shed in September 1935. Note the crank handle for operating the smokebox front 'cod's mouth'. The bottom flap was designed, as shown, for a man to stand on in order to enter the smokebox. *P. Ransome-Wallis/IAL*

CHAPTER THREE

THE STREAMLINER ERA

The 'Silver Jubilee'

It is probable that no appearance of a new UK locomotive had ever caused such a sensation as did the emergence of No 2509 *Silver Link*. That there was to be a 4-hour 'flyer' to Newcastle was widely known, that the engine would be streamlined was generally expected, but most anticipated something like a Pacific version of the 'P2' *Cock o' the North* painted in the usual LNER green with the usual rake of teak coaches.

So when No 2509 first appeared at King's Cross in its silver and grey colour scheme, having been worked up from Doncaster on 13 September 1935 and having made a trip to Cambridge and back on the 14th, the effect on the media was immediate and dramatic. On 22 September No 2509 was used on some unpublicised high-speed braking tests between King's Cross and Doncaster. This confirmed that at high speed the train was unable to stop within normal braking distance and could potentially overrun

In late 1935 the last of the original four 'A4' Pacifics, No 2512 *Silver Fox*, stands on the newly installed Cowans Sheldon vacuum-operated turntable at King's Cross shed. The locomotive is in original silver grey livery with painted name and the 'silver fox' embellishment presented by Samuel Fox and Co. Note on the right the ex-GNR large Atlantic waiting to leave the turntable road. The later No 60017 was always allocated to King's Cross, apart from her last four months at New England. *IAL*

signals, which led to the decision to introduce 'double-block' working for the streamliners, previously only used for the Royal Train. The media impact became even greater one week later when the complete train was presented to the press on Friday 27 September. A special train from King's Cross to Barkston and back was organised to demonstrate the new train to the world's press, accompanied by representatives of the LNER and many of the manufacturers who had supplied equipment for the locomotive and train.

The privilege of working this trip fell to King's Cross driver A. J. Taylor and he and No 2509 maintained the honour of the LNER in spectacular fashion by a demonstration of the fastest sustained running ever seen on rails, attaining no fewer than three new world records for any form of railway traction. It would appear that the Flaman speed recorder fitted to all the 'A4s' was inoperative or had yet to be installed as, after achieving the 112mph, Gresley is reported to have gone through to the locomotive's

You can almost hear that magic chime whistle blow as, in the first week of the 'Silver Jubilee' service in October 1935, No 2509 *Silver Link* warns of her approach as she slows for her station call at Darlington, passing beneath an impressive NER signal gantry with the up train.
Jack Crossley/ Colour-Rail NE 99

No 2512 *Silver Fox* roars through Oakleigh Park station at almost 80mph with only another 8 miles to go to King's Cross with the up 'Silver Jubilee' in the spring of 1936. She still has the short buffers and recessed front coupling that she carried from delivery in December 1935 to October 1936.
F. R. Hebron/IAL

No 2510 *Quicksilver* roars out of Hadley Wood tunnel climbing at 1 in 200 towards Ganwick with the northbound seven-coach 'Silver Jubilee' in the spring of 1937. *IAL*

cab and exclaimed, 'Steady on, old chap, do you know you have just done 112mph? Go a bit easier – we have an old director in the back and he is getting a bit touchy!' Driver Taylor was subsequently interviewed by the press and was reported to have described the 'A4' as, 'The finest engine we have ever had. There is no vibration whatever. We could have gone faster if we had wanted to – we were not out by all means. Quite frankly I didn't think we'd been going much above 90mph and apparently it was smoother on the engine than in the train.'

The distance of 25 miles between Hitchin and Offord was covered at a continuous speed of at or over 100mph, with an average of 107.5mph and a maximum of 112.5mph, achieved twice; the average speed over the 41 miles between Hatfield and Huntingdon was 100.6mph, and the entire distance covered at an average speed of

A spotless No 2509 *Silver Link* is still in original silver grey livery with painted number as she hauls the 5.45pm King's Cross to Harrogate express past New Southgate in this view from 1936-7. The train is overhauling 'K3' No 4008 on a fast goods. *IAL*

In June 1937 No 2509 *Silver Link* stands ready to depart from Grantham station at the head of the up 'Flying Scotsman'. The locomotive had lost the original recessed front coupling and short buffers the previous July after they had been blamed for a fatal accident involving a shunter. On Saturdays this was the regular return working of the locomotive, which had worked the previous day's 'Silver Jubilee' down to Newcastle. *J. A. Whaley/Colour-Rail NE 74*

100mph was 43 miles. The advance in performance made possible by the 'A4' as against that achieved by the 'A3' No 2750 *Papyrus* on her record run some six months earlier was demonstrated for all to see in a most decisive fashion.

The 'Silver Jubilee' was named, following a suggestion by Wedgwood, in honour of the 25th anniversary of the reign of King George V, and the four 'A4s' specially designed to haul the train were given names derived from this title: No 2509 *Silver Link*, No 2510 *Quicksilver*, No 2511 *Silver King* and No 2512 *Silver Fox*. The service began on Monday 30 September 1935, departing from Newcastle at 10.00am and, after one stop at Darlington, arriving at King's Cross at 2.00pm. The return journey left King's Cross at 5.30pm, arriving at Newcastle after the Darlington stop at 9.30pm. Surprisingly, in view of the overnight stabling of the train on Tyneside, the service was worked exclusively by King's Cross locomotives and crews, with only No 2511 *Silver King* out-stationed at Gateshead to provide back-up in case of failure of any of the other three locomotives.

For the first 13 days of the service only No 2509 was available, then on 17 October the second engine, No 2510 *Quicksilver*, was used. No 2509 ran 537 miles each day at a scheduled average speed of 70.4mph start to stop, five days a week, a total of almost 7,000 miles with absolute regularity and without any mechanical troubles, a magnificent performance.

Seen again in early 1938, *Silver Link* gently leans to the curve at New Southgate as she accelerates a north-bound express. *IAL*

The train itself, referred to as 'Set 101', consisted of seven coaches: a twin articulated Brake 3rd, a triplet set with a restaurant car in the middle, and a twin 1st set, increased to eight coaches from February 1938 by the addition of a 3rd to make the Brake 3rd twin into a triplet. The initial seating accommodation for 198 passengers was later increased to 233. The tare weight was 220 tons, again increased to 248 tons in 1938. The coaches were constructed in standard LNER manner, with teak-framed bodies on all-welded steel underframes, initially fitted with standard double-bolster bogies. The external finish chosen was arguably one of the most attractive of any train, the steel panels being covered with a silver-grey Rexine coating. Fairings covered all the underframe equipment and the space between each articulated body was covered by rubber sheeting from solebar level and round over the roof. All the fittings were of stainless steel and the interior included pressure ventilation and heating with double-glazed windows to reduce noise to below 60 decibels. The roofs were sprayed in aluminium paint over a white lead base, with the title 'The Silver Jubilee' fixed to the carriage roofs over a dark-blue background. Supplementary fares were charged at 5 shillings for 1st Class and 3 shillings for 3rd Class passengers.

The 'Silver Jubilee' was an immediate commercial success, and a cost/benefit review of the first year results reported by Wedgwood to the Joint Locomotive and Traffic Committee in October 1936 revealed that the up service had carried an average of 130 passengers, with 143 in the down direction, a load factor of 86%. The income from the supplementary fares alone returned the complete investment in the train, and the gross revenue was as much as six times the operating cost. Overall, Newcastle to London business had grown by 12% since the train had started running, and had thus acted as 'a stimulus to traffic'. The train ran for almost four years between 30 September 1935 and 31 August 1939, the date on which the onset of World War 2 caused all three streamliners to make their last runs.

The 'Silver Jubilee' ran a total of 1,952 journeys, of which No 2509 made 564 trips, No 2510 456 trips, No 2512 409 trips, and No 2511 only 80 trips. Other 'A4s' were responsible for the other 440 runs, with three workings by 'A3s'. There are only 16 recorded instances of locomotive failures on the 'Silver Jubilee', nine involving No 2510 and five No 2509, a miles-per-casualty figure of almost 33,000.

The 'Coronation'

When the 'Silver Jubilee' started running, the LNER announced that, depending on the public reaction, further high-speed trains would be introduced. Following the operational and commercial success of the 'Silver Jubilee', a memo from Wedgwood in October 1936 proposed two new services, one between London and Edinburgh in 6 hours, with one stop at Newcastle, to be called 'the Coronation' and to start from the

With her tender filled to the brim, Haymarket's immaculate Garter blue No 4491 *Commonwealth of Australia* draws the inaugural up 'Coronation' away from Waverley station on 3 July 1937. *IAL*

Newly repainted in Garter blue and displaying her large CPR chime whistle, King's Cross-allocated No 4489 *Dominion of Canada* heads the nine-coach down 'Coronation' out of Hadley Wood Tunnel and towards Ganwick in the summer of 1937. No 4489 had run in photographic grey as *Woodcock* for six weeks between May and June 1937. She was to acquire a CPR bell in March 1938. *F. R. Hebron/Real Photographs*

Summer 1937 timetable, and the other to run between Bradford, Leeds and London, to start in the Autumn of 1937. In fact, a high-speed King's Cross-Edinburgh-Aberdeen train, to a 9-hour overall schedule, had been planned since the spring of 1936, but the idea of an extension to and from Aberdeen was abandoned that October.

As part of the active preparations for the new service the dynamometer car was attached to a run of the 'Silver Jubilee' on 27 August 1936. No 2512 *Silver Fox* had the usual seven-coach load increased to eight vehicles to make a gross trailing load of 270 tons. After passing Grantham, Edward Thompson, then Mechanical Engineer, Southern Area, went through the corridor tender on to the footplate and, during a normal acceleration after passing Stoke summit at about 70mph, reportedly instructed driver Haygreen to 'top a hundred'. The crew were in no way prepared for a record maximum speed attempt, but Haygreen responded with a maximum-effort 35% cut-off burst that took the speed to a record 113mph. Unfortunately, an hour later, near Hatfield, this terrific pounding led to a complete failure of the middle cylinder valve gear. The punishment of the middle cylinder big end had created such overheating as to cause the bearing to disintegrate, and with the extra play the piston had knocked out both cylinder ends! The last 18 miles to King's Cross were taken very gently with a stream of debris being deposited from the locomotive on to the track, and arrival was 7 minutes late. Apparently certain sections of the press were known to be at King's Cross, so a decision was made to press on at caution rather than stop at Potters Bar in order to avoid adverse media comment. No 2509, with driver Sparshatt, took the return northbound run and, in view of earlier events, the closest restraint was put on him to avoid any fireworks, a punctual arrival in Newcastle being achieved with no higher speed than 90mph.

A Newcastle to Edinburgh test run was arranged for Saturday 26 September 1936, when the 'Silver Jubilee' train was available with Gateshead's No 2511 *Silver King*. The

With the 'beaver-tail' observation car bringing up the rear of the ninecoach 'Coronation' set, No 4491 *Commonwealth of Australia* roars up the 1 in 96 of Cockburnspath bank and towards Penmanshiel Tunnel in July 1937. *Real Photographs* T1542

King's Cross-allocated No 4490 *Empire of India* accelerates past Harringay with the northbound 'Coronation'. *Real Photographs* T5200

In June 1938 the light is beginning to fade as Haymarket's No 4489 *Dominion of Canada*, having taken water at Wiske Moor troughs, accelerates the nine-coach down 'Coronation' away from Croft and towards Darlington. She had acquired the CPR bell the previous March. *R. E. Kirkbright/IAL*

With just over 12 miles left to run, King's Cross-allocated No 4492 *Dominion of New Zealand* coasts through Potters Bar with the up 'Coronation' in June 1939, soon after she had acquired her distinctive low-note New Zealand Government Railways chime whistle. *E. R. Wethersett/Real Photographs* 25361

down journey was made in 118 minutes, but on the return rather faster work was attempted and the overall time was only 114 minutes. During this return journey, while climbing the long 1 in 96 gradient up the Cockburnspath bank at a minimum speed of 68mph, the power output of the locomotive was measured in the dynamometer car as between 2,500 and 2,600hp, a new British record.

At the end of December 1936 the first two of a new batch of ten 'A4s' were delivered from Doncaster Works. These were Nos 4482 *Golden Eagle* and 4483 *Kingfisher*. In recognition of their intended use on general express services, rather than exclusively on the streamliners, they were finished in the standard LNER 'apple green' livery, and had their names on cast plates fixed to the side of the smokebox, as had been originally intended for the 'Silver Jubilee' quartet. Four more green 'A4s' were turned out between February and April 1937, Nos 4484-87, named, respectively, *Falcon*, *Kestrel*, *Merlin* and *Sea Eagle*. The next one to appear, in the same month as the Coronation of the new King, was lined out like the other green engines but painted grey for photographic purposes, No 4489 *Woodcock*. This gave the first indication that the new streamliner was not to perpetuate the grey and silver of the 'Silver Jubilee' but, in honour

As the 'A4s' began to be used on general express services, a variety of different liveries emerged. No 4482 *Golden Eagle* shows how attractive the LNER 'apple green' livery looked on the four 'A4s' so decorated in 1936/7. No 4482 carried this livery between December 1936 and January 1938 before being repainted in Garter blue. *LNER/IAL*

The first example of the second batch of 'A4s' was delivered in December 1936. No 4482 *Golden Eagle*, the first 'A4' to be painted in the LNER standard green livery with a lined-out panel on the tender, rests on a shed, thought to be Doncaster. Another first was the use of numerals and letters in gold with red shading. Note also the corridor tender, which previously ran behind 'A1' No 4472 *Flying Scotsman*. The next five 'A4s' had the black smokebox front extended back to the first cladding band on the boiler, ignoring the curve of the smokebox front. Fortunately, wiser counsels prevailed and the last three green 'A4s', Nos 4493-95, had the green restored back to its original graceful curve. *G. Ford/Colour-Rail NE 58*

of the Coronation itself, would carry on the coaches a striking two-tone colour scheme, with 'Garter blue' bodies and 'Cambridge blue' upper panels.

A green locomotive would look out of place with this train, so five of the new engines earmarked for the new service were also painted in Garter blue. In a burst of patriotic fervour the locomotives were to be named after the major countries of the British Empire, so No 4489 was repainted and renamed *Dominion of Canada* at a ceremony at King's Cross on 15 June. The other four engines were numbered 4488-92 and named *Union of South Africa*, *Empire of India*, *Commonwealth of Australia* and *Dominion of New Zealand*. Construction of the green 'A4s' continued after this with No 4493 taking the displaced name *Woodcock* and No 4494 *Osprey*. Thus by the end of August the 17 'A4s' were in three different liveries, four in silver, five in Garter blue and eight in apple green.

No 4487 *Sea Eagle* is seen at Grantham heading the up 'Flying Scotsman' in May 1937, and was one of the five 'A4s' that carried this black-smokebox variant of the apple green livery between March 1937 and February 1938, when Garter blue was substituted with its parabolic curve reflecting the smokebox shape. *T. G. Hepburn/Rail Archive Stephenson*

No 4462 *Great Snipe* heads a long north-bound express past New Southgate in this view from 1938. She carried Garter blue livery from new until wartime black replaced it in October 1942. The future No 60004 became *William Whitelaw* in July 1941. *IAL*

The usual 'A3' Pacific has been replaced by an 'A4' as the 'Northern Belle' departs from King's Cross behind Garter blue No 4467 *Wild Swan* with the first trip of the 1938 season. The 'Northern Belle' was a highly successful week-long land-cruise train formed of 14 overnight 1st Class sleeper accommodation and day coaches that toured LNER (and some LMS) scenic routes in Northern England and Scotland each summer from 1933 to 1939. *E. R. Wethersett/IAL*

The driver of No 4463 *Sparrow Hawk* keeps a close eye on the photographer as the locomotive roars past Ganwick near Hadley Wood on a 13-coach northbound express in 1939. *IAL*

Haymarket's apple green No 4484 *Falcon* heads the 12-coach non-stop up 'Flying Scotsman' towards Grantshouse in the summer of 1937. *E. R. Wethersett/IAL*

In August 1937 a rather grubby apple green No 4486 *Merlin* heads the 12.45pm Aberdeen to Edinburgh express over the Forth Bridge. Haymarket was No 4486's home for 25 years until allocation to St Rollox in May 1962 and finally, for her last 12 months, to St Margarets in September 1964. *E. R. Wethersett/IAL*

On 12 August 1937, six-week-old No 4492 *Dominion of New Zealand* heads the 12-coach non-stop up 'Flying Scotsman' past Ganwick, near Hadley Wood. This view shows how well the Garter blue livery matched the standard teak-bodied LNER stock. *E. R. Wethersett/IAL*

The press run of the new 'Coronation' train took place on 30 June 1937, three days before the first scheduled service. Significantly this was the day after the LMS had made the press run of its new 'Coronation Scot' streamliner, and had just seized the British speed record by the narrow margin of 1mph!

When the 'Coronation' set off from King's Cross on 1st July there must have been many who hoped that the day-old record of the LMS might be surpassed. But No 4489 only managed 109.5mph. With the experience of No 2512 on 27 August 1936 in mind, this was all that could be risked and the LMS retained its record for the time being.

Working the 'Coronation' was a far harder proposition for a locomotive than the 'Silver Jubilee'. With nine coaches instead of seven and a tare weight of 312 tons against 220, the power output required was proportionately greater, but far more important was the working of the one locomotive throughout between King's Cross and Edinburgh. With a scheduled departure from Kings Cross at 4.00pm and from Waverley at 4.30pm, arrivals were exactly 6 hours later at both points. Although remanned *en route*, the 9 tons of coal had to last throughout for 392 miles of hard high-speed running, and on 2 December 1937 No 4490 was so short of coal as to require

No 4489 *Dominion of Canada* stands outside King's Cross Top Shed on 11 March 1938 just after having been fitted with the CPR bell. Originally named *Woodcock* and delivered in shop grey livery, this locomotive was renamed, repainted in Garter blue and fitted with a deep-tone CPR chime whistle after only a month's service on 15 June 1937. Note the stainless steel trim along the lower edge of the side-skirting and the tender. Withdrawn in 1965, the then No 60010 was cosmetically restored at Crewe Works in 1966 and exported to Canada on 10 April 1967, where she now resides in a museum at Delson near Montreal. *Friends of the NRM/ Colour-Rail NE 148*

assistance from Hitchin, followed by No 4492 seven days later. Slight modifications were then made to the tenders to increase capacity.

Locomotive failures were very few. Out of 1,084 runs between 3 July 1937 and 31 August 1939 there were only 13 failures in 1937, 21 in 1938 and 12 in 1939. This equates to more than 9,000 miles per failure, reflecting the fact that the 'Coronation' was a far more arduous task than the other streamlined trains, but still a figure far superior to that typically achieved by today's InterCity 125 sets. Some of the 'A4s' achieved great feats of reliability, in particular No 4491, which worked 48 of the first

51 trips of the service, and No 4489, which worked 18,327 miles in the course of 34 days of continuous working. In the spring of 1939, No 4497 *Golden Plover* made 39 consecutive round trips on the 'Coronation', running 2,358 miles weekly on the high-speed service and achieving a total of 15,327 miles in just over six weeks. On 18 May 1938 the up train was worked throughout by 'A1' No 4473, arriving at King's Cross 16 minutes late.

The 'Coronation' was worked by two nine-coach sets, known as Sets 102 and 103, comprising four articulated twins and the 'beaver-tail' observation car at the rear. The front twin was formed of a Brake 3rd/3rd, then a 3rd/3rd Kitchen, twin 1st and Kitchen 3rd/3rd Brake, followed by the observation car, providing a total of 208 seats, including 16 in the observation car. In the winter months, because much of the running was in the dark, and to give an additional performance margin, the observation car was deleted from the formation. Originally, the 'Coronation' sets were to have followed the 'Silver Jubilee' so far as internal design was concerned, but in January 1937 it was decided that all eight carriages of each set would be of open layout, with all seats (except in the observation cars) reservable; in addition, the provision of two kitchen cars in each set allowed all passengers to be served with meals at their seats. Passenger seating followed the 'Silver Jubilee' standard with 2+1 in 3rd and 1+1 single swivelling armchairs in 1st Class. The view from the observation car was limited in part by the 'beaver-tail' feature, designed to complement the matching shape of the 'A4' Pacific at the front of the train. A supplementary fare of 1 shilling was charged for an hour's occupation of

each of the 16 swivelling armchairs in this vehicle. The 'Coronation' was again a profitable venture for the LNER, with reported results for July 1938 as a profit of 13s 8d per loaded train mile, marginally more than the 'Silver Jubilee'.

The 'West Riding Limited'

On 27 September 1937 the third streamlined train entered service, between Bradford, Leeds and King's Cross. Leaving Bradford Exchange at 11.10am and Leeds Central (after reversal) at 11.31, it was scheduled to arrive at King's Cross at 2.15pm. The return journey departed from King's Cross at 7.10pm, arriving at Leeds at 9.53pm and Bradford at 10.15. This train had a similar set to the 'Coronation' (minus the observation car), being composed of four articulated twin sets of eight vehicles; Set 104 comprised a Brake 3rd, 3rd/Kitchen, two Open 1sts, 3rd Open and 3rd/Kitchen, 3rd Open and Brake 3rd, with seating accommodation for 198 passengers. The external livery was the same

Two of the 'A4s' specially dedicated to the 'West Riding Limited' meet at King's Cross shed in October 1937. Both Nos 4495 *Golden Fleece* and 4496 *Golden Shuttle* were allocated to the London shed from the commencement of the service in September 1937. No 4495 had entered service from Doncaster shed in August 1937 in apple green as *Great Snipe*, before being recalled to Doncaster Works after only two weeks' service in order to be repainted in Garter blue and renamed before being dedicated to the new service. *IAL*

King's Cross-allocated No 2509 *Silver Link* picks up water on Langley troughs with the eight-coach southbound 'West Riding Limited' in the summer of 1938. *Real Photographs T5479*

Doncaster-allocated No 4496 *Golden Shuttle* roars through Potters Bar with the up 'West Riding Limited'. This locomotive became *Dwight D. Eisenhower* in September 1945, and on withdrawal in July 1963 was preserved and donated to the US National Railroad Museum at Green Bay, Wisconsin. *Real Photographs T5478*

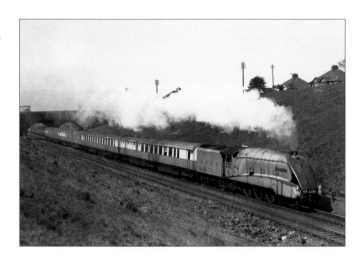

No 4496 *Golden Shuttle* prepares to depart from Wakefield Westgate station with a Leeds/Bradford to London express one morning in 1937. The locomotive was originally intended to be named *Sparrow Hawk* but a more appropriate name was selected when she and No 4495 *Golden Fleece* (the former *Great Snipe*) were selected for use on the 'West Riding Limited' streamliner service. *H. M. Lane/Colour-Rail NE 157*

The fireman is still building up his fire as King's Cross-allocated No 4492 *Dominion of New Zealand*, still carrying her original chime whistle, heads the 7.10pm King's Cross-Bradford 'West Riding Limited' past Potters Bar on 24 June 1938. *K. Nunn/LCGB*

Running a little behind time with a recent snowfall covering the ground, King's Cross-allocated No 4467 *Wild Swan* heads towards Potters Bar with the up 'West Riding Limited' on 28 December 1938. *E. R. Wethersett/IAL*

No 2509 *Silver Link*, by now fitted with cast nameplates and in Garter blue livery, leaves King's Cross for Leeds with the down 'West Riding Limited' on 17 June 1938. *E. R. Wethersett/IAL*

The great man himself: Sir Nigel Gresley is pictured seated in a 1st Class seat in the 'Coronation', stopwatch in hand, timing the train.
A4 Locomotive Society

as the other streamlined sets, with the exception of being lettered 'West Riding Limited' and its vehicles being numbered within the GN section series rather than the East Coast series of the other sets. A fifth eight-vehicle set, No 105, was also constructed at Doncaster to act as 'spare' for the other four.

Two new 'A4' engines, Nos 4495 and 4496, were painted blue and named specially for the service – *Golden Fleece* and *Golden Shuttle* – the names being appropriate to the wool trade of the West Riding.

The 'West Riding Limited' made 968 runs in the almost two years between 27 September 1937 and 31 August 1939. No 4495 made 258 runs, No 4496 277 runs, and No 2509 12 runs. In 1939 No 4495 did 14 consecutive weeks' duty on the 'West Riding Limited', with only three days' break, and No 4496 did 15 weeks with only two days' break. There are only two recorded instances of locomotive failures, reflecting the fact that this was the least arduous of the three streamliner services (giving a miles-per-casualty figure of 90,000); there were ten substitutions by eight 'A1s', one 'A3' and one 'V2', with the maximum recorded late arrival being only 11 minutes.

By this time the Running Department was experiencing some inconvenience in having to allocate engines of the appropriate colours to the streamlined trains and in having green 'A4s' that it was not desired to use on any of them. So in the autumn of 1937 the decision was taken to paint all the 'A4' engines in blue, and the last engines to be repainted were No 4493 in July 1938 (green to blue) and No 2511 in August 1938 (silver to blue). A blue engine would, of course, look equally good at the head of a standard East Coast express in the traditional varnished teak livery or at the head of the 'Silver Jubilee' train.

The three streamlined trains made a total of 4,004 runs, of which engine No 2509 was the most prolific performer, making 608 runs (15% of the total). The total mileage run was 1,128,112, providing an overall miles-per-casualty figure for these dedicated high-speed trains of 17,626, a figure of which most modern fleet engineers would be most envious. Curiously, one 'A4' never featured on any of the streamliners, No 4903 *Peregrine*, built in July 1938.

1936: a significant year

In addition to the achievement of the British speed record on 27 August, 1936 proved to be a memorable year for Nigel Gresley personally. On 21 February he became President of the Institution of Mechanical Engineers, and the University of Manchester also chose to award him an honorary degree of Doctor of Science (DSc). This was followed by the announcement later in the summer in the King's Birthday Honours List that he was to receive the honour of a knighthood for his services 'as engineer and speeder-up to the LNER.', as *The Times* happily expressed it.

Other streamlined services

In November 1936, together with the stock for the 'Coronation' and 'West Riding Limited' services, a new set of stock was authorised for the Liverpool Street to Norwich service. From the beginning this 'East Anglian' service was referred to as a high-speed service, which it was in style if not journey time. At 2hr 15min over the distance of 115 miles, the 'East Anglian' was only marginally faster than the best of the other services on the route and could not therefore justify a supplementary fare; it became the least profitable of the LNER high-speed trains. Weight restrictions on the GE lines precluded any use of Pacifics, so the six-coach non-articulated teak-panelled train, built at York, was worked by a special 'A4-style' cosmetically streamlined pair of 'B17' 4-6-0s, Nos 2859 *East Anglian* and 2870 *City of London*.

In June 1935 a high-speed service was proposed for the Hull to Liverpool service via Doncaster, Sheffield and the Woodhead route to Manchester and beyond. This would have had a four-coach train including catering facilities. Clearly, as with the 'East Anglian', high-speed in this instance was a relative term, and again 'B17' class engines would have been probable if the service had ever materialised.

The 100th Gresley Pacific

After the 'West Riding' pair of 'A4s', the next to be turned out was No 4497 *Golden Plover*. It was noticed that this was the 99th Gresley Pacific, and this generated a suggestion to the LNER by Mr K. Risdon Prentice of the RCTS that the next 'A4', as the 100th of that illustrious line, should be named after the designer. Engine No 4498, completed at Doncaster on 30 October 1937, was therefore worked over to Marylebone on 26 November to be named by William Whitelaw, the Chairman of the Company, as *Sir Nigel Gresley*. It was one of the greatest honours ever conferred on a British locomotive engineer while still in office.

No 4498 was the 100th Gresley Pacific and was named *Sir Nigel Gresley* in honour of her designer. Here she stands at Belle Isle waiting to back down to King's Cross station and being passed by 'A3' No 2599 *Book Law* climbing the grade with a northbound express. *IAL*

The 50th Anniversary of the 'Flying Scotsman' train and the entry into service of a new set of coaches for this prestigious service was celebrated on 30 June 1938. As ever the LNER organised a spectacular media event with the invited guests conveyed between King's Cross and Stevenage in a specially restored 1888 train hauled by Stirling 'Single' No 1. At Stevenage the guests transferred to the new 'Flying Scotsman' set, hauled by 'A4' No 4498 *Sir Nigel Gresley*. Here both trains are posed side by side at Stevenage. *LNER/IAL*

Sir Nigel Gresley crosses a southbound express onto the up Leeds fast line at Dringhouses, south of York, in this view from 1938. The locomotive carries Garter blue livery with painted numbers and letters, replaced by stainless steel numbers and letters during a general overhaul at Doncaster between November 1938 and January 1939.
A4 Locomotive Society/ IAL

At any time Manchester Central station was an unusual setting for an 'A4', but in March 1938 No 4498 *Sir Nigel Gresley* is seen at the head of an LNER touring exhibition train there. This train was displayed with an 'A4' at various East Coast locations, but the Manchester visit is thought to have been motivated by the award of an honorary degree to the CME by Manchester University.
IAL

It is 11.30 on a spring morning in 1939 as No 4489 *Dominion of Canada* gets ready to leave Leeds Central station with the up 'West Riding Limited' streamliner. This service originated at Bradford and was hauled to Leeds by a brace of 'N2s' where, after reversal, the 'A4' was attached for the 2hr 44min non-stop sprint to King's Cross.
H. M. Lane/Colour-Rail NE 205

CHAPTER FOUR

THE WORLD SPEED RECORD

The build-up

On 3 March 1938 the 28th 'A4' Pacific entered traffic. No 4468 was named *Mallard* and was different from her predecessors in being fitted from new with a Kylchap exhaust and double chimney. This was an almost identical arrangement to that already been fitted to 'A3' No 2751 *Humorist* and the 'W1', No 10000, and resulted from the experience gained by Gresley from this arrangement, which had already been applied to the 'P2' 2-8-2 locomotives in 1934. The 'W1' had been so equipped in 1935, almost as a 'last ditch' final improvement to a troublesome experiment, prior to its complete rebuilding in 1937. Since 1932, No 2751 had been used for a variety of experiments designed to cure the inherent problem of large-boilered locomotives working on short cut-offs – drifting exhaust steam obscuring the driver's forward view. In July 1937, *Humorist* emerged from Doncaster plant fitted with a Kylchap exhaust and double

A nearly new No 4468 *Mallard* heads the up 'Yorkshire Pullman' near Brookmans Park in the summer of 1938. The Pullman trains routed via the West Riding were regular work for the two Doncaster - allocated 'A4s', Nos 4468 and 4903 *Peregrine*, both of which were fitted with a double chimney from new.
George R. Griggs/IAL

Mallard leaves King's Cross on 17 June 1938 with the 5.50pm Harrogate express. Driver Duddington is at the regulator, as he would be just over a fortnight later when the engine reached 126mph down Stoke bank.
E. R. Wethersett/IAL

chimney as part of these continuing experiments. The installation proved to be only partially successful, as in January 1938 further modifications were made with the fitting of wing deflectors and the removal of the beading from the chimney. The wedge-shaped front end of the 'A4s' totally solved this problem by other means, although the installation on No 4468 was not immediately repeated with the next four 'A4s' into traffic in March, April and May 1938, Nos 4469, 4499, 4500 and 4900. By June the installation on No 4498 was delivering sufficiently good results for the final three 'A4s' – Nos 4901, 4902 and 4903 – all to be delivered with the full Kylchap installation. As with most LNER locomotives involving experimental installations, No 4468 was kept close to Doncaster Works for observation reasons and was allocated to Doncaster shed.

In their search for continual improvements, particularly after the results of the high-speed braking trials on 22 September 1935, the Gresley team appreciated that the existing vacuum braking system had significant practical limitations in that the application of the brakes at the rear of the train was slow and, in the case of a sudden brake application, could be both violent and could cause snatching. Double-blocking south of York was no more than an interim expedient, and from 1935 experiments had been made with suburban quadruple sets in which Westinghouse quick-service application (QSA) valves had been fitted. These were a development of the Direct Acting (DA) valve developed by the GWR. With this system, during a brake application air is admitted to the train pipe of each coach direct from the atmosphere, instead of through the driver's brake valve. While it does not increase the power of the application, it applies the brakes at the rear of the train much more quickly than otherwise, and considerably shortens the stopping distance. The results were encouraging and, somewhat surprisingly, the 1937 'East Anglian' was the first set to be fitted from new. In due course 'Coronation' Set 103 was similarly fitted, together with automatic

On 3 July 1938, only seven hours before achieving the world speed record, No 4468 *Mallard* passes Potters Bar with the northbound test train. Note the double chimney – she was the first 'A4' to be so fitted – the venerable NER dynamometer car and the reduced six-coach 'Coronation' set. No 4468 spent her first five years allocated to Doncaster shed before five years at Grantham, then King's Cross from 1948 until withdrawal in 1963.
Kenneth Leech/ Colour-Rail NE 57

slack-adjusters, and this was the set selected for a series of brake trials on alternate Sundays during the spring and early summer of 1938.

Towards the end of June 1938 Sir Nigel Gresley was apparently discussing some of the results of these tests with one of his technical staff, Norman Newsome. What transpired during that conversation has been reported by George Dow, at that time working for the publicity department of the LNER. Apparently Sir Nigel leaned back in his chair and enquired when the next test was to be held; on being told that it was the next Sunday, he is quoted as saying, 'Do you think we could go faster than the LMS?'

Newsome reportedly replied, 'I think so, if we could go to Barkston and if we put the dynamometer car on and take one twin off.'

'Will you fix it up then for next Sunday?' was Gresley's response, and so was set the scene for 3 July 1938.

Plans were made with the utmost secrecy and were only known to a handful of higher officials. The locomotive was carefully selected, being the four-month-old Kylchap double-chimney-fitted 'A4' No 4468 *Mallard*; her driver, Doncaster-based Joe Duddington, and his regular fireman, Tommy Bray, accompanied by Inspector Jenkins. Noted train performance recorder Cecil J. Allen was invited to ride on the 'brake test', but, unaware of the real purpose of the run and having an aversion to working on a Sunday, he declined the invitation.

3 July 1938

The usual Westinghouse testing team were apparently surprised and curious to see that on Sunday 3 July the usual 'Coronation' set provided for the test train was reduced to only three twin sets, supplemented by the ex-NER dynamometer car, that it was headed by an 'A4' that they had not had previously, No 4468 *Mallard*, and that it was manned by a crew with strong Yorkshire accents rather than their more usual Cockneys. They were also surprised to note that their run was to be extended from its usual Peterborough terminus to Grantham and Barkston.

The usual tests were conducted between King's Cross and Peterborough, and only after the extended run to Barkston was the true nature of the day's events revealed. The Westinghouse staff were offered taxis back to Peterborough if they did not wish to participate in the record attempt, an offer they all declined. At Barkston the triangle was used to reverse the train and run-round the locomotive and dynamometer car. Shortly after 4.00pm driver Duddington opened the regulator of No 4468 and they began the run that was to make history. Duddington later became something of a celebrity, and I can do no better than report his own account of the day's events given to the BBC following his retirement in April 1944:

On 3 July 1938 the 'brake test' special heads north through Potters Bar hauled by No 4468 *Mallard*. Six hours later she would establish the new and still standing World Speed Record for steam traction. Note the dynamometer car ahead of the reduced six-coach spare 'Coronation' set. *L. J. Burley/ Gresley Society*

'It was one Sunday in July 1938. That was the day that the grand streamlined engine *Mallard*, that I had driven ever since it came new from the shops in March that year and looked upon as almost my own property, made, with me driving her and Tommy Bray as my fireman, the world's record for high-speed steam locomotive running. The record has not been equalled to this day [it still stands 70 years later]. We made it between Grantham and Peterborough on the LNER main line. I'd taken expresses along at, well, 60, 70 or 80mph, but this day we were really going out to see just what we could do.

'When we drew away from Grantham we had besides the train a dynamometer car containing a speed recorder and other instruments. I accelerated up the bank to Stoke summit and passed Stoke box at 85. Once over the top I gave *Mallard* her head and she just jumped to it like a live thing. After 3 miles the speedometer in my cab showed 107 miles per hour, then 108, 109, 110 – getting near 'Silver Jubilee''s record of 113, I thought,– ''I wonder if I can get past that'' – well, we'll try, and before I knew it I the needle was at 116 and we'd got the record. They told me afterwards that there was a deal of excitement in the dynamometer car and when the recorder showed 122mph for a mile and a half it was at fever heat. ''Go on, old girl'', I thought, ''we can do better than this.'' So I nursed her and shot through Little Bytham at 123, and in the next one

and a quarter miles the needle crept up further – 123.5, 124, 125 and then for a quarter of a mile, while they tell me the folks in the car held their breaths, 126 miles per hour. That was the fastest a steam locomotive had ever been driven in the world – and good enough for me, though I believe if I'd tried her a bit more we could have got even 130.'

After easing somewhat for the bend at Essendine a strong aniseed smell was noticed, indicating overheating of the middle big end, so the run came to a somewhat premature end at Peterborough. The damage sustained was no more than overheating, sufficient for the white metal to have run out of the big end brasses, and the locomotive was soon repaired and returned to traffic. An Ivatt GN 'Atlantic' worked the train forward from Peterborough to King's Cross and the press, who had been alerted to the record speed, had to content themselves with photographs inside the dynamometer car of the paper speed trace made by the recording equipment. So the world record speed for steam propulsion was wrested from Germany, who had claimed 124.5mph, and the British record was taken from the LMS. Note that in his 1944 report driver Duddington claimed 126mph, although the LNER in 1938 only claimed 125mph; however, 126mph is the speed shown on the plaques that were mounted on the locomotive in 1948. As Cecil J. Allen had declined the invitation to ride on the train there was no experienced

No 4468 draws an express into the terminus at King's Cross. No 4468 was unusual in that she had three detail differences from the previous 'A4s': her Kylchap double blastpipe and chimney, the designation 'Class A4' shown beneath the front number, and the lack of the usual access plate below the nameplates. No 4468 remained at Doncaster shed until a transfer to Grantham in 1943 before reaching her final home at King's Cross in 1948. *IAL*

train-timer aboard, so we have only the dynamometer car rolls as evidence. Apparently, despite the rolls showing a peak of 126mph, Gresley refused to use this as the basis for a record claim because it was only a peak; in his view a claim must be for a sustained speed over a distance. In the immediate aftermath of the record run a number of congratulatory telegrams were received by Sir Nigel, including one from Sir William Stanier. Lady Wedgwood, wife of the LNER Chairman, sent a brief telegram, reported by Geoffrey Hughes in his biography of Gresley as 'Three cheers for the Mallard. LMS out for a duck.'

Echoing the views of Driver Duddington, Gresley himself believed that a speed of 130mph was feasible for a Kylchap-equipped 'A4', and there is some evidence that a further attempt was being planned for September 1939, an event forestalled by the outbreak of the Second World War, then the death of Gresley himself in April 1941.

CHAPTER FIVE

'A4s' AT WORK ON THE LNER IN THE 1930s AND '40s

By July 1938 all 35 'A4s' were in service, and were allocated to King's Cross (11), Grantham (2), Doncaster (3), Gateshead (8), Heaton (1) and Haymarket (10). Apart from the four engines rostered to the three daily high-speed services, the remainder were utilised on ordinary express services. From the summer of 1937 the non-stop 'Flying Scotsman' had been rostered to 'A4s', replacing 'A1s' and 'A3s' after nine years of successful summer workings. Again the 'A4s' soon established a similar degree of reliability as had been demonstrated on the high-speed services. One typical example is of King's Cross-based No 4492 *Dominion of New Zealand*, which worked the 'Flying

Photos of 'A4s' on sleeping car trains are, of necessity, somewhat rare. Here Garter blue No 4465 *Guillemot*, the first 'A4' into traffic in 1938, hauls the heavy 16-coach 'Aberdonian', the 7.30pm King's Cross to Aberdeen sleeping car express, past Brookmans Park in the London suburbs. *Photomatic/IAL*

Scotsman' for ten consecutive days from 18 July 1937, then had two days 'off' as pilot to the 'Coronation', working to Peterborough and back. Then the non-stop working was resumed for no fewer than 44 consecutive days, including the usual Sunday workings on an ordinary express. Eight more days were worked when the 'Flying Scotsman' made a stop at Newcastle, so in all the engine worked 62 trips and more than 24,000 miles between London and Edinburgh, 52 of which were on consecutive days! Not to be outdone, No 4489 *Dominion of Canada* ran 18,327 miles in seven weeks in the summer of 1939, which included 34 days of continuous use entailing one week on the 'Coronation', four weeks on the non-stop 'Flying Scotsman', one week on the 'West Riding Limited' and finally one week on the 'Coronation' again.

The two Grantham 'A4s', Nos 4466 *Herring Gull* and 4494 *Osprey*, worked the down 'Aberdonian' sleeping car express between Grantham and Edinburgh, returning the following day on the up 'Night Scotsman' sleeper. The Doncaster allocation was used principally on West Riding Pullman car expresses. The Heaton engine, No 4464 *Bittern*, was diagrammed for the 8.15am Newcastle to King's Cross service on Mondays, Wednesdays and Fridays, returning on each following day's 10.00am 'Flying Scotsman'. The Gateshead allocation worked three turns to King's Cross, increased to four each summer, in addition to standing pilot to the King's Cross engine working the 'Silver Jubilee', after which the locomotive concerned worked the 11.08am Newcastle to Edinburgh train, returning with the 5.12pm Edinburgh to Newcastle (Glasgow-Leeds) express.

On 11 August 1939 No 4490 *Empire of India* approaches Alnmouth, Northumberland, past a fine array of ex-NER semaphore signals with the 12-coach up non-stop 'Flying Scotsman'. No 4490 was one of five 'A4s' dedicated to the 'Coronation' high-speed service and had, after nine months' service from King's Cross, moved to her home for the next 24 years at Haymarket in March 1938. Later, as No 11/60011, she continued to be a favourite for the non-stop workings until they ceased in 1961. *KRM 043761*

Another of the five 'Coronation'-dedicated 'A4s' was No 4492 *Dominion of New Zealand*. Here she brings the up non-stop 'Flying Scotsman' under the magnificent signal gantry at the north end of Newcastle Central station in 1938. For the first eight months of the 'Coronation' service No 4492 was based at Haymarket before a move in March 1938 to King's Cross for the next 25 years, apart from a two-year spell at Grantham between 1948 and 1950. *KRM 045702*

The Second World War

With the outbreak of war on 3 September 1939 the UK railways came under government control for the second time in the 20th century, with overall direction being exercised by a Railway Executive under the control of the Ministry of War Transport. The most obvious sign of change for the public was the implementation of a new Emergency Timetable consequent upon a 60mph maximum speed limit, with many passenger trains cancelled and long-distance expresses consolidated with greatly extended journey times.

The three streamliner services made their last runs on Thursday 31 August 1939 and, initially, the King's Cross stud of 14 'A4s' was put into store until December, when two were moved to Grantham. Other sheds kept their 'A4s' at work; Haymarket retained seven locomotives, with eight at Gateshead, one at Heaton, four at Doncaster and one at Grantham. No 4468 *Mallard* remained at Doncaster shed until October 1943, when she moved to Grantham.

As early as July 1939 the Ministry of Transport had consulted the railways with an estimate prepared by the War Office indicating a potential military requirement for 800 locomotives, subsequently reduced to 100. Although most of this requirement was for freight and shunting locomotives, the impact was immediately felt across the locomotive fleets of the 'Big Four'. Recently withdrawn locomotives were reinstated and there was a general downwards cascade, with many services facing extended journey times so that

In August 1946 Grantham-allocated No 2510 *Quicksilver* retains her wartime black livery as she works an up Leeds to London express north of Hatfield. The tender lettering had been changed from the plain 'NE' designation acquired in October 1943 to 'LNER' during a general overhaul at Doncaster in April 1946. She had to wait until October 1947 to regain her Garter blue livery. *E. D. Bruton/ Colour-Rail NE 100*

At outbreak of war the 12 King's Cross 'A4s' were initially put into store, but the demands for motive power meant that they soon drifted back into service. 'A4s' at other sheds remained in traffic, and here a very grimy No 4495 *Golden Fleece* of Grantham shed has just taken water at Werrington troughs, north of Peterborough, as she heads a northbound express in 1940. The zigzag sign opposite indicates the commencement of the water troughs for southbound trains.
G. J. Jefferson/IAL

On 4 September 1943 No 4498 *Sir Nigel Gresley* heads a short Cambridge to London empty stock train past Shepreth, just south of Cambridge. The locomotive had been 'de-frocked' and had acquired plain black livery in February 1942, although she retained her stainless steel LNER tender lettering, barely recognisable under a thick coat of grime.
E. R. Wethersett/IAL

smaller locomotives than those previously employed could be utilised. For long-distance expresses the contrary was mostly the case, with many services packed to capacity and having extra coaches added. Trains departing from King's Cross were frequently packed, with hundreds of standing passengers; trains of more than 20 coaches became common, with 25 being recorded on several occasions. With such pressure on resources it is not surprising that the King's Cross stud of 'A4s' was soon drifting back into a service requiring a very different utilisation from their former speciality of lightweight high-speed services. On 4 December 1939 a new augmented East Coast timetable was introduced and all the members of the King's Cross stud were again fully employed.

Although wartime reports of train running were of necessity much curtailed, some did emerge, such as on 5 April 1940, when No 2509 *Silver Link* took 25 coaches – 850

Pictured on 23 July 1941, during the course of a general repair at Doncaster, No 4462 *Great Snipe* had become *William Whitelaw* and had most of the side skirting removed. All subsequent 'A4' visitors to Doncaster had the full treatment, but No 4462 retained this hybrid arrangement, albeit briefly, until arrival at Haymarket shed on 24 July, when the shedmaster immediately had the front portion removed. The locomotive surprisingly retained the Garter blue livery until the end of October 1942 before wartime black became the order of the day. *IAL*

By 5 July 1941, in the course of a light repair at Doncaster, the full 'de-frocking' was applied to No 4487 *Sea Eagle*, but again she retained Garter blue until a general repair the following September. This locomotive became *Walter K. Whigham* in October 1947. For her first two years of service No 4487 had no fewer than five homes before becoming a permanent King's Cross resident, apart from a 30-month spell at Grantham between 1945 and 1948. *IAL*

Ex-works off a general repair on 25 September 1945, No 4496, the former *Golden Shuttle*, became *Dwight D. Eisenhower*, and was the first 'A4' to have her Garter blue livery restored prior to display to the directors at their monthly meeting at Marylebone on the 26th. On 2 June 1946 No 4496 stands on Peterborough New England shed; in the following November it became No 8. *E. R. Wethersett/IAL*

tons gross – on the 1.00pm King's Cross to Newcastle service, with only 15 minutes being booked against the locomotive through to Newcastle. Shortly afterwards No 4901 *Capercaillie* was recorded taking a train of 21 coaches – 730 tons gross – south from Newcastle at an average speed for more than 25 miles of almost 76mph, with a maximum of 78.5mph. In contrast, No 4468 *Mallard* was noted passing Darlington in January 1940 at the head of a down goods train, but two years later worked the southbound 'Flying Scotsman' and, despite leaving Newcastle 14 minutes late, regained 8 minutes to Grantham with a train loaded to well over 700 tons gross.

Inevitably, with the huge demands of wartime service, the intense utilisation, 'common-user' deployment and reduced standards of maintenance, the Gresley Pacifics, and the 'A4s' in particular, became progressively run down as the war progressed. The Gresley-conjugated valve gear did not respond well to lack of maintenance and severely 'off-beat' locomotives became common. In contrast, Haymarket depot managed to retain its seven 'A4s' on regular out-and-home workings with top link crews, and, despite staff and material shortages, the shed's locomotives were kept in such a satisfactory condition that their standard of performance was sustained at a very high level, with very few failures. O. S. Nock records a Newcastle to Edinburgh hauled by Haymarket's No 4483 *Kingfisher* in the summer of 1945 when a 17-coach, 610-ton train was worked up to 84mph.

The death of Gresley

As the war progressed Sir Nigel Gresley began to exhibit the classic signs of overwork and his health deteriorated. Chronic bronchitis set in and his heart began to fail. He managed to make it to York on 19 February 1941 to see the unveiling of both his last steam locomotive, No 3401 *Bantam Cock*, and his first electric locomotive, Bo-Bo No 6701. A month later he was not well enough to attend the first showing at Waterloo of the new 'Merchant Navy' class Pacific *Channel Packet*, designed by his former assistant Oliver Bulleid. Shortly afterwards, on 5 April 1941, he died at his home at Watton-at-Stone.

The LNER Chairman, Sir Ronald Matthews, apparently approached both the Southern, in an effort to entice back Bulleid, and the LMS, to query the availability of R. C. Bond. However, he was unsuccessful, and the choice of successor fell to the Doncaster Mechanical Engineer, Edward Thompson. Thompson required changes to the LNER locomotive policy set by Gresley and agreed with Matthews a review of the three-cylinder policy to be undertaken by an independent adjudicator, Sir William Stanier of the LMS! Apparently the report was rather non-committal, and Stanier did not actually condemn the conjugated valve gear, merely commenting that he would not use it himself. From the many changes implemented by Thompson, not least of which was the extensive and unsympathetic rebuilding of Gresley's very first Pacific, No 4470 *Great Northern*, it soon became clear that the era of Gresley Pacific domination of the East Coast route had begun to go into eclipse.

The end of No 4469

On 29 April 1942 No 4469 *Sir Ralph Wedgwood* (the former *Gadwall*) was unlucky to be in the wrong place at the wrong time. Ex-works after a general overhaul completed only 12 days earlier, No 4469 was being run in on local trains, stabling overnight in York North shed. Unfortunately this was the date chosen by Hitler's Luftwaffe for the so-called 'Baedecker' raid on York, and the 'A4' took the full blast of a high-explosive bomb on its right side. The remains arrived at Doncaster on 18 May and the locomotive was condemned on 20 June. Only the tender survived, being attached in 1945 to Thompson's 'A2/1' class No 3696 (later No 507 *Highland Chieftain*).

The LNER renumbering

In 1943 Thompson announced a scheme of renumbering the whole locomotive fleet. The block of numbers 580 to 613 inclusive was reserved for the 34 surviving 'A4' locomotives, to be applied in their order of construction. However, in order to accord appropriate preference to the Company's Chairman, Deputy Chairman, the director in charge of the Locomotive Committee and Chief General Manager the proposed

The final wartime condition of the 'A4s' is shown in this January 1944 view of No 4466 just off a general repair and after renaming from *Herring Gull* to *Sir Ralph Wedgwood*. This was to replace the earlier locomotive of the same name, No 4469, the former *Gadwall*, which had been destroyed in an air raid on York shed on 29 April 1942. The plain black livery with plain 'NE' lettering looked good when clean, a condition unfortunately only achieved when immediately ex-works! *LNER/IAL*

Nos 596, 608, 609 and 611 were changed to 3, 2, 1 and 4 respectively. Owing to the priorities of wartime operations it was not practicable to commence the general renumbering until 1946, and between 26 January and 19 April five of the class were altered to Nos 585-88 and 605. By May wiser counsels had prevailed and the 'A4' number sequence had been completely recast as Nos 1 to 34.

The first three were unaffected, but honour to the Chairman from 1923 to 1938 was paid by giving No 4's name to William Whitelaw, and the Chief General Manager's name dropped back to No 5. Two esteemed ex-officials took over Nos 6 and 7, and the remaining celebrity engine took No 8. Nos 9 to 13 were the five engines selected in 1937 for hauling the 'Coronation', and the remainder then assumed Nos 14 to 34 in ascending order of original running number. This differed from their construction sequence and gave the new Nos 18 to 22 earlier places than they would otherwise have received. Despite most renumbering being undertaken at running sheds, the 'A4s', with their metal cut-out numbers, posed problems and were therefore generally left until their next works visit.

In May 1946 No 587 *Kestrel* heads a Newcastle to King's Cross express at Peascliffe, just north of Grantham. The former No 4485 was renumbered on 18 April in a sequence intended to run from 580 to 613, in the same sequence as construction, but by 26 May was again renumbered as No 26. Only Nos 585, 587, 588 and 605 ever had these numbers applied. This locomotive became *Miles Beevor* in November 1947, and in 1967 donated parts, including driving wheels, towards the restoration of No 4498 *Sir Nigel Gresley*. *T. G. Hepburn/IAL*

Left:
In a wintry scene from 1946 the former No 4489 *Woodcock*, now No 10 *Dominion of Canada*, heads a 16-coach northbound express near Hadley Wood. The locomotive is still in wartime black livery but regained the stainless steel number and lettering in May 1946 before full Garter blue in November, just prior to nationalisation. The locomotive acquired the ex-CPR bell in 1938, and carried it until a double chimney was fitted in November 1957. *F. R. Hebron/IAL*

In 1947 Grantham-based No 32 *Gannet* heads north past New Barnet with the 15-coach 5.30pm King's Cross to Newcastle express. The former No 4900 had been renumbered in November 1946 and became No 60032 in June 1949. No 32 was only one of a few 'A4s' never to carry 'British Railways' on its tender. *IAL*

Nationalisation and the 1948 Locomotive Exchanges

On 1 January 1948 the railways were nationalised and the LNER ceased to exist. At nationalisation the 34 'A4s' were evenly spread between two Eastern Region sheds (King's Cross with nine locomotives and Grantham with ten), one North Eastern shed (Gateshead, with eight locomotives), and one Scottish Region shed (Haymarket, with seven locomotives). Early in the year five 'A4s' moved from King's Cross to Grantham and five others, significantly including the three ER-allocated Kylchap double-chimney 'A4s', all with corridor tenders, moved south in return.

Shortly after nationalisation it was announced that, in order to produce in as short a time as possible indications as to the most desirable features to incorporate in future standard designs, a series of locomotive interchange tests were to be undertaken. These were not intended to be a contest between locomotives of similar types, which, it was acknowledged, had been designed to fulfil the specific requirements of their respective regions. It was also acknowledged that these trials would be of a broad nature as the

tests were to be conducted under normal operating conditions and without any special preparation of the locomotives. It was arranged to take straight out of traffic engines that had run between 15,000 and 25,000 miles since their last general repair, and this was the only stipulation laid down as far as actual locomotive selections was concerned.

Three categories of locomotives were designated for the trials: Express Passenger, General Purpose, and Freight. In each category it was intended that one class of locomotive would be selected from each of the 'Big Four' pre-nationalisation companies, except that in the Express Passenger category the LMS would be represented by both the 'Princess Coronation' and the newly rebuilt 'Taper Scot', and as the SR had no modern heavy freight locomotives both the 'WD' 2-8-0 and 2-10-0 types would be used in the freight category. A further anomaly was that in the General Purpose category the three Class 5 locomotive types drawn from the GWR, LMS and LNER would be joined by the SR 'West Country' design of Class 7 Light Pacifics. The routes chosen for the Express Passenger type trials were to be, in order of operation:

On 12 February 1948 newly nationalised No 29 *Woodcock* makes a smoky departure from Platform 6 at King's Cross with the 1.10pm Leeds express. As the safety valves begin to lift, the fireman looks down to check the injector overflow in an effort to forestall a bout of blowing off, which would cause unpleasant conditions for the crew in Gasworks Tunnel. No 29 had regained her Garter blue livery in July 1947 and finally sported the identity of her new owner and the BR trial purple livery in July 1948. *C. C. B. Herbert/IAL*

The fireman keeps a suspicious eye on the photographer as King's Cross-allocated No 6 *Sir Ralph Wedgwood* heads a long unfitted Class F freight from Cambridge to Ferme Park through a station on the Cambridge to Hitchin line in the summer of 1948. The former No 4466 *Herring Gull* became No 60006 in December 1948. *R. F. Dearden/IAL*

April	ER, King's Cross to Leeds
Early May	WR, Paddington to Plymouth
Late May	LMR, Euston to Carlisle
June	SR, Waterloo to Exeter

By 1948 the ER had 25 Thompson Pacifics of Classes 'A2/1', 'A2/2' and 'A2/3' and a handful of brand-new Peppercorn 'A2s'. Given the mixed performance of the Thompson Pacifics, it is not surprising that the choice of ER Express Passenger type fell to the 'A4'. Initially No E21 *Wild Swan*, No 25 *Falcon* and No 26 *Miles Beevor* were chosen, but Doncaster succeeded in substituting the entire ER fleet of Kylchap 'A4s', so that No E22 *Mallard*, No 60033 *Seagull* and No 60034 *Lord Faringdon* were selected, all of which fortunately satisfied the mileage criteria and had been transferred from Grantham to King's Cross shed in March and April. The fourth Kylchap 'A4', No 60005 *Sir Charles Newton*, was a North Eastern Region locomotive, based at Gateshead. In each series of tests, four days of running were to be preceded by four days of familiarisation trips on the designated routes and trains for the 'foreign' locomotives and their crews.

For the ER tests No 60034 *Lord Faringdon* was selected and ran without problems. For all of the 'away' trips the ER management deliberately chose the celebrity No E22 *Mallard*, by now newly adorned with the boiler-side plaques proclaiming her holding of the World Speed Record for steam traction. The running staff at King's Cross shed had protested that *Mallard* was not their best 'A4' at that time and strongly suggested the use of another of the class, but higher authority insisted, with unfortunate results. *Mallard* was moved over to Old Oak Common for the preliminary WR familiarisation trips, which began on 27 April, but she did not even complete the first round trip, being failed with a hot middle big end at Savernake on the way back to London on the 28th. No 60033 *Seagull* was quickly worked over to Old Oak Common and successfully completed all of the WR runs. For the two weeks of LMR trials the third 'A4', No 60034 *Lord Faringdon*, was used, and again ran without any problems. The SR familiarisation trips commenced on 1 June with the 'Atlantic Coast Express' to Exeter, worked by No 60033 *Seagull*. Unfortunately the weak point of the 'A4s' was again apparent, and No 60033 was failed just short of Exeter. By now repaired, *Mallard* was worked over to Nine Elms and made a splendid run with the first dynamometer car run on 8 June, but the jinx

On 22 April 1948 Grantham-allocated No 32 *Gannet* heads north at Greenwood with the 4.05pm express from King's Cross to Cleethorpes, which she will work to Peterborough. The former No 4900 would become No 60032 in June 1949. The locomotive is in Garter blue with cut-out numbers, which she had acquired in May 1947. *A. C. Cawston/IAL*

On 22 April 1948 No 17 *Silver Fox* proudly displays the pre-war headboard as she passes Greenwood box with the 12-car 'Yorkshire Pullman', the 4.45pm from King's Cross to Leeds, Harrogate and Hull. The locomotive still retains Garter blue livery and the stainless steel numbers and letters that she had regained in September 1947, together with the 'silver fox' emblem. *A. C. Cawston/IAL*

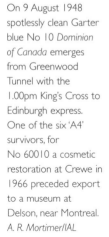

On 9 August 1948 spotlessly clean Garter blue No 10 *Dominion of Canada* emerges from Greenwood Tunnel with the 1.00pm King's Cross to Edinburgh express. One of the six 'A4' survivors, for No 60010 a cosmetic restoration at Crewe in 1966 preceded export to a museum at Delson, near Montreal. *A. R. Mortimer/IAL*

While not exactly common, use of 'A4s' on freight trains was not exceptional, and on 18 May 1948 Grantham-allocated No E8 *Dwight D. Eisenhower* approaches Potters Bar with a long up Class C freight. The former No 4496 retained her LNER livery until acquiring BR Blue in June 1950. *J. C. Flemons/IAL*

struck again coming back to London on the 9th when she was failed at Salisbury. The final two test runs on the SR were undertaken by newly repaired No 60033 *Seagull*, without any further problems.

When the test results were published the 'A4s' emerged as the most economical in both coal and water consumption of any express passenger locomotive tested. Although there were wide variations in the way individual drivers interpreted the test conditions and train schedules, the handling of the 'A4s' must inevitably have reflected the apprehension felt by their drivers after the series of inside big end failures to which their charges were all too publicly prone. Despite this they were the only locomotives whose drivers consistently drove at full regulator with short cut-offs, the results being a vindication of the efficiency of the Gresley front end arrangement.

Despite the ER authorities' clear preference for the Kylchap double chimney locomotives for use during the Locomotive Exchanges, they were surprisingly slow to seek any conversions beyond the four locomotives delivered with this equipment in

1938. Gresley had previously indicated that he would seek further conversions once the patent, and thus the need to pay significant royalties, had expired in 1941, but obviously the exigencies of wartime and the death of Sir Nigel, together with the antipathy of his

On the first day of route familiarisation runs on the Western Region for the 1948 Locomotive Exchanges, No 22 *Mallard* ran hot at Savernake while working the 1.30pm Paddington to Plymouth service. In LNER Garter blue livery and with stainless steel numbers, but with her new owner's name now carried on her tender, she is seen on Reading shed the following day, 28 April 1948, departing light engine for home at King's Cross before a quick visit to Doncaster for repairs. *M. W. Earley/IAL*

The replacement for *Mallard* was No 60033 *Seagull*, also in Garter blue but with painted numbers and the 'British Railways' legend on the tender. Here she takes the 1.30om Paddington to Plymouth service past West Drayton on the third day of the actual WR tests, 6 May 1948. Note the ex-GWR dynamometer car at the front of the 14-coach train. *P. Ransome-Wallis/IAL*

The following day, 7 May, was the last of the WR tests, and No 60033 *Seagull* rests in the unfamiliar surroundings of Paddington station after arriving with the 8.30am Plymouth to Paddington express. After the failure of *Mallard* on the first day of the tests, *Seagull* worked the remaining seven days without any problems, acquitting herself very well. *C. C. B. Herbert/ IAL*

On the first northbound LMR familiarisation run on 17 May 1948 No 60034 *Lord Faringdon* makes an unassisted climb past Scout Green on the 1 in 75 ascent of Shap. *Canon Eric Treacy/IAL*

On her second northbound run on the 'Royal Scot' on 19 May, *Lord Faringdon* coasts past Leyland and approaches Farington Junction with a 15-coach load. This locomotive fitted with Kylchap exhaust and double chimney from new in 1938, was formerly No 4903 and had been named *Peregrine* until March 1948. The name of the former LNER Deputy Chairman was transferred from an ex-GCR 4-6-0, which had just been scrapped. *IAL*

Monday 24 May was the first day of actual LMR tests, with the ex-LMS dynamometer car now attached to the down 'Royal Scot'. Here No 60034 takes water at speed from Dillicar troughs as she approaches Tebay and the assault of Shap. *Overend Agency/IAL*

The first Southern Region familiarisation run took place on 1 June 1948. Here No 60033 *Seagull* departs from Waterloo with the 10.50am to Ilfracombe, which she was intended to work to Exeter, but unfortunately she ran hot before reaching her destination. The, by now repaired, No 22 *Mallard* was substituted for the next down run. *IAL*

successor Thompson towards much of the Gresley inheritance, had prevented any further developments in this direction. The Running Department had long held the view that the Kylchap cowls restricted access to the tubes for cleaning and had resisted any further conversions. In fact, in order to minimise the risk of problems caused by shortage of steam, it became standard practice at King's Cross with every single-chimney 'A4' that had worked beyond Doncaster to have the fire thrown out on its return, the tubes rodded and the tubeplate scraped to remove any accumulation of 'birds' nests'. That this was unnecessary on their three Kylchap 'A4s' because the blast kept the tubes clear does not appear to have percolated through to 'official' thinking on the subject. It was to take a further nine years before the persistence of the King's Cross shedmaster, Peter Townend, eventually overcame this resistance and the conversion of the remaining 30 'A4s' was authorised.

After the failure of *Seagull* no time was lost in working the newly repaired *Mallard* over from King's Cross to Nine Elms shed. On 3 June No 22 poses alongside a 'Lord Nelson' 4-6-0 on Nine Elms shed, prior to working the 10.50am to Ilfracombe. *Mallard* then worked two days of familiarisation runs and the first two days of actual tests before running hot and failing at Salisbury on the up trip on 9 June, being replaced again by *Seagull* for the last two days of tests. *IAL*

The day of the first actual test run on the Southern Region was 8 June. No 22 *Mallard* departs from Waterloo for Exeter with the 10.50am to Ilfracombe, the 'Atlantic Coast Express', with the ex-GWR dynamometer car at the front of the train. *IAL*

CHAPTER SIX

THE EAST COAST MAIN LINE IN THE 1950s AND '60s

The return of the non-stop

The first tentative sign of a return to pre-war conditions was the re-instatement from 31 May 1948 of the summer-only non-stop working of the 'Flying Scotsman' service. The first runs were made by Nos 60034 *Lord Faringdon* (northbound) and 60009 *Union of South Africa* (southbound). On 12 August disastrous flooding affected eastern Britain and the East Coast Main Line suffered washouts at 12 locations between Berwick and Dunbar. Trains were diverted over the 'Waverley' route and thence via Kelso to Tweedmouth, which, in addition to being almost 16 miles longer, included the 1 in 70 climb to Falahill (for which banking was usual for loads of more than 400 tons), the 25mph line speed over the single line between St Boswells and Kelso and the 45mph thence to Tweedmouth. A water stop at Galashiels was also required, as the first troughs were 91 miles away at Lucker. After 12 days the Haymarket crews responded to the challenge, and on 24 August driver Stevenson in charge of the up 'Flying Scotsman' succeeded in making the unassisted run to Lucker troughs without stopping for water, and the challenge of maintaining the non-stop run over the 408 miles of the amended route had been established. On subsequent days the Haymarket crews managed to achieve the non-stop run on no fewer than 17 occasions up to the resumption of the normal route on 22 September, including a run on 15 September by No 22 *Mallard*.

By the end of 1948 principal East Coast engine workings had been reorganised to facilitate 'single-home' (out and back in a day) workings, with locomotives based at King's Cross, Grantham, Gateshead and Haymarket sheds being changed at Grantham and Newcastle. This facilitated the allocation of regular crews to engines and led, despite often indifferent coal supplies, to a general improvement in locomotive appearance, morale and thus performance. In May 1949 a test run from King's Cross to Edinburgh and back was organised to assess the feasibility of enhanced schedules, and during the return journey No 60017 *Silver Fox* reached a maximum speed of 102mph descending from Stoke. Although the 'A4s' were obviously ready and able, the track was less so, and it was to be a further two years before 90mph speeds were to be authorised over certain sections of the main line.

By the summer of 1951 things had begun to slip back and, in an effort to restore matters, the redoubtable ER Motive Power Superintendent L. P. Parker had the engine allocations and workings further reorganised. All of the ER allocation of 'A4s' were concentrated at King's Cross, with the 'A3s' and 'A1s' moved out to Grantham, Doncaster and Leeds Copley Hill. Thus began the regular association of King's Cross 'A4s' with specific drivers, which continued almost to the end of East Coast steam and the widespread dieselisation of the early 1960s. There was some competition for the most famous engines like *Silver Link*, which went to Ted Hailstone, newly arrived at King's Cross from the West Riding. He was possibly the most dedicated to 'his' No 14, and had special pins made for the middle big end oil feed, to give it a little more than the standard, together with specially polished buffers, which Top Shed was careful to retain whenever No 14 was required to visit Doncaster. *Mallard* was shared by J. Burgess and A. Smith; Burgess soon retired and J. Howard moved over from *Walter K. Whigham* to

27 August 1948 was the centenary of the 'Flying Scotsman' train, and here No 60029 *Woodcock* accelerates the newly restored non-stop working past Holloway, with 12 coaches in tow. Extensive flood damage to the main line caused the service to be diverted from 13 August via Tweedmouth, Kelso and Galashiels to the 'Waverley' route, extending the journey to a record-breaking 408.6 miles. Initially, stops for banking assistance and water brought an end to non-stop working, but the Haymarket crews soon responded to the challenge and from 24 August made nine southbound and eight northbound non-stop runs before the service ceased with the winter timetable. No 60029 was one of only four 'A4s' to acquire the short-lived BR purple livery, and on 27 August, with driver Stevenson in charge, made the third successive non-stop northbound run. *BR/IAL*

No 60020 *Guillemot* heads the up 'Flying Scotsman' through York in February 1950. The locomotive still carries LNER Garter blue livery with 'British Railways' added to the tender, and displays the pre-war LNER headboard, the train being a mixture of Gresley and Thompson vehicles. The former No 4465 was always a Tyneside-allocated loco and carried the same non-corridor tender throughout her 26 years in traffic.
E. D. Ginz/IAL

On 8 March 1950 Grantham-allocated No 60026 *Miles Beevor* heads the up 'Northumbrian' towards Stoke Tunnel. The former No 4485 *Kestrel* has by now acquired the BR dark blue livery she carried between 1949 and 1952. The 'Northumbrian' was the 8.00am Newcastle to London express, which disappeared when the up morning 'Talisman' service was introduced in 1957.
J. P. Wilson/IAL

On 1 August 1951 BR dark blue-liveried No 60027 *Merlin* takes water from Wiske Moor water troughs north of Northallerton with the down 'Capitals Limited' for Edinburgh. Always a Scottish-allocated locomotive, the former No 4486 carries on the boiler side the naval plaques donated in May 1946.
E. R. Wethersett/IAL

On 23 August 1952 No 60017 *Silver Fox* heads the 13-coach up 'Norseman' express past Retford goods yard. The former No 2512 was always a King's Cross locomotive, except for her last four months of service, and carried the BR dark blue livery for two years until December 1952. Unfortunately the stainless steel boiler cladding straps had by now been painted over, only the stainless steel 'silver fox' emblems remaining uncovered. The 'Norseman' ran in connection with the Bergen Line sailings to Newcastle Tyne Commission Quay. The sixth, seventh and eighth coaches are a Gresley three-car articulated dining car set. *Tom Lewis/IAL*

replace him. The trio of Howard, Smith and *Mallard* established a fine reputation for performance, possibly only overshadowed by Bill Hoole and No 60007 *Sir Nigel Gresley*.

1951 was the year of the Festival of Britain, and in an attempt to raise general standards the non-stop was accelerated to a 7hr 20min schedule and transferred to the advance portion of the 'Flying Scotsman', which was named 'The Capitals Limited'. By May 1952 a further series of three trial runs was undertaken between King's Cross and Doncaster. No 60003 *Andrew K. McCosh* was used, with Ted Hailstone in charge,

accompanied by Inspector Jenkins, of *Mallard*'s famous record-breaking run fame. The runs established a new schedule for the 156 miles of 154.5 minutes with 350 tons, 163.5 minutes for 400 tons and 168 minutes for 500 tons.

The work of Kenneth Cook

The other change in 1951 was a general reorganisation of the mechanical engineering management within the BR regions. From Swindon to Doncaster, as M&EE of both the

No 60033 *Seagull* stands ready to depart from King's Cross on 'The Capitals Limited' non-stop express to Edinburgh in 1949. This train ran in the summer timetable from 1949 to 1952, departing from both stations at 9.30am (9.45am in 1952). In 1953 it became 'The Elizabethan' and continued to run each summer until 1961. The locomotive still carries LNER Garter blue livery but with the addition of 'British Railways' on the tender. The former No 4902 was one of the four 'A4s' fitted with a double chimney from new. *J. F. Aylard/ Colour-Rail BRE 280*

Eastern and North Eastern Regions, came K. C. Cook. He was an expert in workshop practice and was fortunate in still having on his staff at Doncaster Bert Spencer, who had played such a prominent part in the revitalisation of the original 'A1' Pacifics in the 1930s. It was some time before Cook's influence began to be apparent, but it can be said at once that his arrival at Doncaster was a great day for the Gresley Pacifics. Cook set about a systematic programme of rehabilitation by eliminating those features of detailed design that had proved sources of weakness. A supplier was found to provide the type of optical alignment equipment that had been used for many years at Swindon to achieve a high degree of accuracy when setting up frames and motion. This permitted pins and bearings to be machined to much finer tolerances, and the Gresley conjugated

In 1952 No 60004 *William Whitelaw* passes a freight in the down goods loop and heads for home at Haymarket with the down 'Flying Scotsman' north of Berwick on Tweed. The train has now acquired a Mk 1 BSK at the front, but is still largely formed of Gresley and Thompson vehicles. *Eric Treacy/IAL*

In the same year No 60004 gets away from Glasgow Queen Street up the 1 in 41 gradient to Cowlairs, assisted in rear by an 'N15' 0-6-2T, with a Glasgow to King's Cross express. *E. R. Wethersett/IAL*

valve gear in particular was now assembled with such precision that the wildly syncopated exhaust beats that had become so characteristic of the three-cylinder locomotives became a thing of the past. Locomotives overhauled at Doncaster now ran with the quietness and precision of well-oiled sewing-machines. The inside big end bearings, for so long the Achilles heel of the Gresley Pacifics, were also modified by Cook; the Gresley marine big end was modified with the Swindon form of white metal bearing, with the same very high standards of surface finish and methods of lubrication. This proved to be totally effective and the problems of wear in the conjugated valve gear and overheating of the middle big end were totally overcome, Thus the Gresley Pacifics entered into a positive Indian Summer of their lives.

The final enhancement to the 'A4s' came, not as the result of Cook's work at Doncaster, but through the persistence of the King's Cross shedmaster, Peter Townend. Throughout the 1950s the sheds maintaining the single-chimney 'A4s' fought a not always totally effective battle against the tendency, particularly when supplied with less than ideal coal supplies, for the engines to be reported by their crews as 'short of steam'. The modifications concentrated on variations in the size of the blastpipe orifice, which, by 1957, had been progressively reduced to a diameter of 5⅛ inches. This had led inevitably to significantly increased blastpipe pressure and showed that the lesson of the double chimney was being missed, in that the considerable improvement in steaming was obtained by a reduction in exhaust pressure. Contemporarily with this work, at

Swindon S. O. Ell was rejuvenating the ex-GWR 'King' and 'Castle' classes by fitting double chimneys and higher-degree superheat with excellent results. Despite this, the BRB and ER CME authorities resisted requests for further double-chimney modifications to the 'A4s'. After four years of fruitless requests from King's Cross, eventually a local initiative was set up to undertake comparative tests between single-chimney and double-Kylchap 'A4s' working round trips for five days each between King's Cross and

On 15 June 1954 No 60015 *Quicksilver*, in typically smart Top Shed condition, heads the 11-coach 8.50am King's Cross to Leeds and Bradford 'White Rose' express under the North London Line viaduct past Belle Isle and towards Copenhagen Tunnel, on its non-stop run to Doncaster. The former No 2510 had acquired the BR Brunswick green livery in November 1951. *Eric Treacy/IAL*

In a typical pose Driver Bill Hoole is in charge of his own No 60007 *Sir Nigel Gresley* as they storm out of Hadley North tunnel with the 8-car Down 'Tees-Tyne Pullman' on 6 July 1954. This train was the post-war successor to the 'Silver Jubilee', although it had a more leisurely 190 minute schedule to its first stop 188miles away at York.
A. C. Cawston/IAL

Doncaster. This was done in order to demonstrate the known economy of the Kylchap system in a form that would convince the General Manager that the costs of conversion could quickly be recovered.

The tests demonstrated that the saving on coal was of the order of 6-7lb per mile, and the cost of the alterations just over £200 per locomotive. The licence costs for the Kylchap design before the patent expired in 1941 had been in the order of £400-500 per locomotive, so the reluctance of Nigel Gresley to authorise such significant expenditure before that date was understandable. The subsequent 16-year wait for the authorisation of such an obvious enhancement was less explicable. The tests proved conclusive and the remaining 'A4s' were all converted between 1957 and 1958, the last to emerge from Doncaster, on 27 November 1958, being No 60032 *Gannet*.

Under a fine array of semaphore signals No 60007 *Sir Nigel Gresley* restarts the up 'Flying Scotsman' from Newcastle Central station in 1955. The train is now in a uniformly smart carmine-and-cream livery but still includes some Thompson catering vehicles. The former No 4498 had to wait until December 1957 to have its Kylchap exhaust and double chimney fitted.
Eric Treacy/IAL

In August 1955 No 60024 *Kingfisher* heads the up 'Elizabethan' non-stop Edinburgh to London express up the 1 in 96 of Cockburnspath bank towards Penmanshiel Tunnel. The train is still composed entirely of Thompson coaches. *IAL*

The 'Elizabethan'

In 1953 the summer non-stop was renamed the 'Elizabethan' in honour of the new Queen. The first down run was made by No 60028 *Walter K. Whigham*, and the up train had Haymarket's favourite 'A4' No 60009 *Union of South Africa*. By 1954 the schedule for this prestige service had been reduced to 390 minutes, an average of just over 60mph throughout. Haymarket shed tended to keep whichever of its 'A4s' was in the best condition specifically rostered to the 'Elizabethan', and some of its locomotives undertook long periods of continuous working, such as in 1960 when No 60027 *Merlin*

On 26 August 1960 Haymarket's spotless No 60027 *Merlin* has her tender piled high with coal as she passes Grantshouse with the up 'Elizabethan' non-stop express for London. *R. Leslie/IAL*

In early September 1961, No 60022 *Mallard* departs from Edinburgh Waverley station with one of the very last non-stop southbound 'Elizabethan' express runs for King's Cross. No 60022 worked the very last northbound 'Elizabethan' trip on the 9th of that month. *J. T. Inglis/Colour-Rail SC 535*

made 74 runs, with 46 consecutive runs between 22 June and 6 August. A further 21 consecutive runs were made between 21 August and 10 September. Despite the introduction of the Type 4 diesels from 1958 and the 'Deltics' in 1961, there was insufficient new motive power available to cover all the work, so the 'Elizabethan' continued to be 'A4'-hauled to the end of the 1961 season, the last runs being made on 9 September. The honour of hauling the last steam-hauled northbound 'Elizabethan' fell to No 60022 *Mallard*, with Haymarket's choice for the last southbound service being yet again No 60009 *Union of South Africa*.

On 2 August 1961 the down 'Elizabethan' nears the end of her non-stop journey from King's Cross at Craigentinny, hauled by King's Cross-allocated No 60033 *Seagull*. Ready to depart from the carriage sidings is the empty stock for the 5.15pm Edinburgh to Glasgow Queen Street service, hauled by an English Electric Type 4 (later Class 40) diesel-electric. *W. S. Sellar/IAL*

On 17 September 1956 BR introduced the new 'Talisman' 4.00pm express between London and Edinburgh in both directions. The service had a 265-minute schedule to its first stop 268 miles away at Newcastle. Here No 60021 *Wild Swan* poses with the new train at Greenwood. Note the ex-'Coronation' articulated twin Open 1st included in the set as the second and third vehicles. *BR/IAL*

The inaugural run of the eight-coach afternoon 'Talisman', the 4.00pm from Edinburgh, passes Portobello West box hauled by Haymarket's immaculate No 60031 *Golden Plover*. Note the specially burnished front buffers and coupling. The Gresley articulated twin Open 1st can also be seen again. *IAL*

On 22 June 1959, No 60004 *William Whitelaw*, by now fitted with Kylchap exhaust and double chimney, heads the afternoon 'Talisman' out of Penmanshiel tunnel and beneath the A1 road. During engineering works in the 1970s this tunnel collapsed and a new diversion had to be constructed to bypass it. *H. Harman/IAL*

The 'Talisman'

The pre-war 4.00pm King's Cross to Newcastle and Edinburgh 'Coronation' streamliner often loaded to capacity, but it was to be 17 September 1956 before a late-afternoon Anglo-Scottish service was to reappear. From this date, 4.00pm 'Talisman' departures from King's Cross and Edinburgh were introduced on a 6hr 40min schedule. These became regular 'A4' turns, although the Peppercorn 'A1s' also frequently appeared. One link with the pre-war streamliners was maintained in that one of the Gresley articulated twin 1st Class saloons was included in both 'Talisman' sets of eight, later nine, coaches.

With the June 1957 timetable remodelling and acceleration, new morning Anglo-Scottish fast expresses were introduced that required the sets of roller-bearing-fitted coaches to undertake, by returning on the afternoon 'Talisman' services, a complete round trip of 786 miles daily, a UK first. Between September 1957 and September 1958 the morning services were extended to and from Perth and became 'The Fair Maid', reverting to the morning 'Talisman' when these services were cut back to Edinburgh from that date.

Other regular 'A4' work

Other regular 'A4' turns throughout the 1950s were to Leeds and back with the 'Yorkshire Pullman', to Newcastle on the 'Tees-Tyne Pullman', and to Edinburgh and Glasgow on the 'Queen of Scots' and 'Talisman'. The East Coast Pullman services maintained a tradition going back to 1923 when the newly formed LNER had inherited contracts with the Pullman Car Company entered into by the GER in 1920. Other than on boat trains, the GER Pullman services had been unprofitable, so the LNER redeployed the cars to new 'Queen of Scots' and 'West Riding Pullman' services. When in 1935 a Hull portion was added, the Leeds and Bradford train became the 'Yorkshire Pullman'.

From 1956 onwards the greater reliability demonstrated by the Gresley Pacifics was reflected in a greater reliance on through engine workings to Newcastle. One of the

On 16 September 1957, No 60015 *Quicksilver* heads the 7.45am down 'Fair Maid' approaching Greenwood box. This service was the new morning 'Talisman', extended to Perth, an experiment that survived for only 12 months to September 1958. *J. Aylard/IAL*

On 20 October 1959 the 8.30am departure from Edinburgh, the morning 'Talisman', nears the summit of Cockburnspath bank hauled by Haymarket's No 60027 *Merlin*. Note the naval plaque fitted to the boiler side in May 1946. The former No 4486 had acquired her Kylchap exhaust and double chimney in February 1958. *H. Harman/IAL*

Not all 'A4' work was on top link expresses, and fill-in turns to Cambridge were common. Here on 14 August 1954 No 60006 *Sir Ralph Wedgwood* carries Class 2 headlamps as it heads the 2.21pm King's Cross to Cambridge semi-fast away from Welwyn Garden City. The train is formed of two Gresley articulated 'Quad-art' high-capacity suburban sets. The former No 4466 *Herring Gull* was renamed in January 1944. *J. N. Faulkner/IAL*

Another regular King's Cross 'A4' duty was 'No 266 Down', the afternoon Scotch Goods from King's Cross. During 1957 No 60028 *Walter K. Whigham* heads the long train past Abbots Ripton, north of Huntingdon.
Eric Treacy/IAL

'No 39 Up', the 9.44am Delavel to Holloway empty stock, was frequently double-headed as far as Clifton sidings at York, and here in 1955 Gateshead's No 60020 *Guillemot* is covering for the booked 'A2', being assisted by York's 'B16' No 61432 as they haul the very long train towards Thirsk.
IAL

On 9 April 1955 No 60002 *Sir Murrough Wilson* heads for home at Gateshead after working the empty stock of an earlier arrival at Newcastle Central from London. To save line occupation through Newcastle station she has been attached to a 'K1' hauling a rather assorted up Class J freight. Apart from six weeks at King's Cross in 1943 the former No 4499 *Pochard* was always a Gateshead locomotive and was never paired with a corridor tender.
K. Field/IAL

During 1955, No 60017 *Silver Fox*, a King's Cross locomotive for 28 years, puts on a fine display of exhaust as she climbs the 1 in 107 gradient out of Gasworks Tunnel and past Belle Isle with a Leeds and Bradford express.
Eric Treacy/IAL

In 1956 No 60018 *Sparrow Hawk* heads north from York with the 8.45am Bristol to Newcastle express. The former No 4463 was always a Tyneside-allocated locomotive and never ran with a corridor tender. This train was a Heaton 'A3' diagram, so the 'A4' is substituting for another Class 8. *Eric Treacy/IAL*

On 29 July 1955 Haymarket's No 60031 *Golden Plover* has some assistance when climbing Cockburnspath bank with the 10.10am 'Junior Scotsman' from Edinburgh to London. The St Margarets 'B1', No 61191, was attached to save a path south as she was required in Newcastle to power an unbalanced northbound Bank Holiday relief. Putting the pilot inside the train engine was a North Eastern practice.
C. J. B. Sanderson/IAL

On 3 September 1957 No 60024 *Kingfisher* heads west from Edinburgh Waverley station with the 4.15pm express for Aberdeen. Apart from brief visits to King's Cross and Doncaster in 1937 and 1939, respectively, the former No 4483 was always a Scottish-allocated locomotive and was one of the last two 'A4' survivors in regular service to September 1966. *P. Groom*

hardest workings was not even a passenger train but 'No 266 Down', the afternoon King's Cross to Niddrie fast fully-fitted goods, worked by a King's Cross top link crew with their own regular 'A4' to Newcastle. Punctuality was thought to be enhanced by the scheduled arrival time in Newcastle being just sufficient for a well-earned pint or two to be consumed before closing time – as long as the arrival was punctual!

From the winter of 1958, Type 4 2,000hp diesels began to be rostered to East Coast expresses on diagrams of some intensity. The new diesels proved troublesome, however,

in many cases due to lack of staff familiarity and the less-than-ideal facilities provided initially for maintenance of this relatively 'high-tech' motive power. Because trains were still heated by steam, the diesels were provided with oil-fired steam generators (and even water scoops for replenishing their water supplies on the move), which proved troublesome and a frequent source of failures. The only available replacements were steam locomotives, and there are many recorded instances of these successfully replacing non-available diesels on diagrams of much greater intensity than had ever been

On 30 May 1960 a very smartly turned-out No 60030 *Golden Fleece* heads the eight-car down 'Tees-Tyne Pullman' north of Finsbury Park. After the first month at Doncaster, the former No 4495 *Great Snipe* was always allocated to either Grantham, for three spells in 1939-42, 1942-50 and briefly in 1957, or King's Cross. *P. Groom*

On 8 October 1960 Haymarket's No 60012 *Commonwealth of Australia* brings the 9.30am Glasgow Queen Street to King's Cross express through Princes Street Gardens as she approaches Waverley station. *S. Rickard/IAL*

In the spring of 1962 No 60011 *Empire of India* restarts the seven-car 11.00am Glasgow Queen Street to King's Cross 'Queen of Scots' all-Pullman service from Edinburgh Waverley station. The former No 4490 was always a Scottish-based 'A4' and moved in June 1962 to Aberdeen, surviving until May 1964. *IAL*

contemplated in previous times. For example, between 30 November and 20 December 1958 No 60030 *Golden Fleece* worked the 'Flying Scotsman' from King's Cross to Newcastle, then returned on the 5.00pm return service on 13 days, and, with other services included, worked 9,018 miles during an 18-day period. During the week ending 2 April 1960, No 60022 *Mallard* worked this same turn on six consecutive days before another return trip to Newcastle on the seventh day, covering 3,752 miles in the process.

The sight of two 'A4s' at Grantham as late as 3 August 1962 was unusual. Here No 60006 *Sir Ralph Wedgwood* runs into the station at the head of the 3.50pm King's Cross to Leeds relief and passes No 60022 *Mallard* heading south with the 4.28pm Doncaster to King's Cross service. Note that the first two coaches of the northbound train are Gresley articulated stock. *J. M. Rayner/IAL*

On 4 August 1962, *Mallard* is now in charge of the 7.30am Leeds/Bradford to London 'West Riding' as it departs from Doncaster, being given precedence over a following 'Deltic'-hauled train. Behind the train, in the up yard, is the Doncaster up pilot, locally based 'A1' No 60144 *King's Courier*. *J. Cupit/IAL*

On 18 August 1962 No 60017 *Silver Fox* heads the 'Anglo-Scottish Car-Carrier' past High Dyke and towards Stoke tunnel. The first six vehicles are specialised double-deck car-carrying vans, the passengers travelling behind in conventional coaches. This service was the forerunner of the later 'Motorail' service and operated in the summer between Perth and King's Cross Goods. *Les Perrin/IAL*

No 60018 *Sparrow Hawk* departs from Newcastle Central with the nine-coach 8.40am King's Cross to Edinburgh express on 11 August 1962. The former No 4463 was always a Tyneside locomotive, was always coupled to the same non-corridor tender, and had only a further ten months of service left. Note that most lines have third-rail electrification for the ex-NER North Tyneside suburban electric services.
J. M. Rayner/IAL

With the smoke abatement restrictions in force at King's Cross behind him, the fireman on No 60025 *Falcon* has begun to build up his fire as the locomotive passes Finsbury Park with the ten-coach down 'Yorkshire Pullman' in June 1953. The former No 4484, which retained its single chimney until 1958, had acquired Brunswick green livery in December 1952, its eighth different livery during a 26-year period in traffic. *J. B. McCann/Colour-Rail BRE 1323*

In all-too-typical Gateshead condition No 60020 *Guillemot* has very slim patronage as she calls at Drem with the 6.20am York to Edinburgh express in 1955. Apart from 10 months at Heaton in 1945, the former No 4465 spent all of her 26 years of service allocated to Gateshead shed. She did not acquire a double chimney until November 1957. *J. G. Wallace/Colour-Rail SC 500*

The low March sun glints off the side of No 60020 *Guillemot* as she departs from York with an up express in 1957. The superheater has yet to have an impact on the exhaust steam as it provides a spectacular white cloud of exhaust against the cool spring air. *W. Oliver/ Colour-Rail BRE 843*

The 60mph permanent speed restriction on the 1 in 96 gradient has posed no problems for No 60023 *Golden Eagle* as she climbs Cockburnspath bank towards Penmanshiel Tunnel with the up 'Flying Scotsman' in August 1955. The former No 4482 retained her single chimney until 1958 and was halfway through a 21-year residence at Gateshead when photographed.
J. G. Wallace/Colour-Rail SC 501

In May 1957 No 60005 *Sir Charles Newton* passes Chaloner's Whin Junction, just south of York, with an up express, heading towards Church Fenton rather than up the old main line towards Selby. The former No 4901 *Capercaillie* was one of the only four 'A4s' to receive a double chimney as built in 1938. It was renamed *Charles H. Newton* in August 1942, amended to *Sir Charles Newton* in June 1943. Charles Newton had replaced Ralph Wedgwood as Chief General Manager of the LNER and the change in 1943 reflected the knighthood that he had just been awarded. Before transfer to Scotland in 1963, No 60005 had spent all her time allocated to Gateshead shed.
W. Oliver/Colour-Rail BRE 1526

In June 1957
No 60023 *Golden Eagle* approaches Chaloner's Whin Junction on the up fast line with one of the first runs of the new 'Morning Talisman' Edinburgh to King's Cross express. The service had begun as an afternoon fast service in both directions on 17 September 1956, expanded to a morning pair the following June. In September these morning trains were extended from Edinburgh to Perth and became 'The Fair Maid', but were cut back to Edinburgh again in September 1958, reverting to the title 'Morning Talisman'. *W. Oliver/Colour-Rail BRE 1932*

In November 1957 No 60011 *Empire of India* climbs the lower portion of Cockburnspath bank with the 12-coach up 'Junior Scotsman', a relief to the main 'Flying Scotsman' train. Note that the former No 4490 is carrying a reversed headboard on the lower middle lamp bracket and that, almost ten years since nationalisation, this important train still has some Gresley coaches included in its fully carmine-and-cream formation. *C. J. B. Sanderson/ Colour-Rail SC 1281*

In June 1958 a very smart No 60031 *Golden Plover* takes water at Newcastle Central with the Saturday 9.00am King's Cross to Edinburgh train. The headboard is being carried for the return working and should have been reversed. The former No 4497 was based at Haymarket shed in Edinburgh for the first 25 years of her service, before a final three years at St Rollox in Glasgow. *R. Shenton/Colour-Rail BRE 1650*

In July 1958 a very smartly turned out No 60016 *Silver King* stands ready to leave York on an up express. The former No 2511 was a Tyneside resident at Heaton or Gateshead for her first 28 years of service before spending her last 18 months in Scotland at St Margarets and Aberdeen. The double chimney was fitted during a general overhaul at Doncaster in June 1957.
C. J. B. Sanderson/ Colour-Rail BRE 1850

In February 1960, long-term Haymarket resident No 60012 *Commonwealth of Australia* storms through fresh snow as she climbs Cockburnspath bank with the 11.00am Edinburgh to King's Cross express. The former No 4491 acquired her double chimney in July 1958.
C. J. B. Sanderson/ Colour-Rail SC 774

In July 1961, No 60026 *Miles Beevor* accelerates the 8-coach down 'Tees-Tyne Pullman' past New Southgate. Introduced in September 1948, this Pullman service took over the premier tea-time Newcastle departure slot of the pre-war 'Silver Jubilee'. Note how effectively the locomotive's wedge-shaped front end lifts the exhaust clear of the driver's sight line.
A. C. Sterndale/ Colour-Rail BRE 1578

With less than 5 miles to run, No 60021 *Wild Swan* coasts past Wood Green in July 1961 with an up Newcastle express. The carriage shed in the background is now the Bounds Green depot serving modern East Coast Main Line services. Beyond the sidings and shed, the Hertford loop line curves away to the right. The former No 4467 was named *Kestrel* until November 1947 and acquired her double chimney in April 1958. *M. Smith/Colour-Rail BRE 2005*

In July 1961 a very smartly turned out No 60028 *Walter K. Whigham* still has 356 miles to run as she nears the summit of Cockburnspath bank with the up 'Elizabethan' non-stop express for King's Cross. Note how the tender has been filled to the brim with coal for this 392-mile journey. The locomotive's excellent external condition is partly a result of a Royal Train working on 8 June, when, for the wedding of the Duke of Kent, she worked between King's Cross and York, returning from Malton. For the first ten years of her service the former No 4487 was named *Sea Eagle*, until renamed after the last LNER Deputy Chairman.
C. J. B. Sanderson/ Colour-Rail SC 777

In September 1961 No 60013 *Dominion of New Zealand* climbs the 1 in 107 gradient past Belle Isle and the exit from King's Cross shed with the down 'Tees-Tyne Pullman' for Newcastle. Note the large five-note NZGR whistle that the locomotive carried throughout her 26 years in traffic. The tall overbridge in the background carries the North London line over the lines out of King's Cross and has recently been altered out of all recognition by a new viaduct constructed to carry Eurostar trains out of St Pancras International station. *A. C. Sterndale/ Colour-Rail BRE 1575*

Off the beaten track

On 29 August 1956 No 60004 *William Whitelaw*, heading the 14-coach 10.10am Edinburgh to King's Cross 'Junior Scotsman' express, has been diverted via Carlisle and here storms through Hexham station *en route* back to Newcastle and her regular route south. After four years at King's Cross, Gateshead and Heaton, the former No 4462 *Great Snipe* became a Scottish-based locomotive for her remaining 25 years of service.
I. S. Carr/IAL

Also during 1956, diverted off the main line via Darlington by engineering operations, Gateshead's No 60005 *Sir Charles Newton* brings an up express round the goods lines avoiding Stockton station. From the LM stock the train could be a Newcastle to Bristol service. The former No 4901 *Capercaillie* was another of the four 'A4s' fitted with Kylchap exhaust and double chimney from new.
J. W. Armstrong/IAL

On 23 September 1956, engineering works caused East Coast services between Peterborough and Doncaster to be diverted via Lincoln. Lincoln Central station is thronged with locospotters attracted by the spectacle as No 60034 *Lord Faringdon* heads a diverted northbound Anglo-Scottish express. The former No 4903 *Peregrine* was the last 'A4' to be constructed, and carried the Kylchap exhaust and double chimney from new. *Eric Oldham/IAL*

The 7.53am Sunderland to King's Cross service, Heaton Turn 1 and booked for an 'A1', has been covered on this grey day in 1959 by Gateshead 'A4' No 60016 *Silver King*. Unfortunately, despite the modest seven-coach load the locomotive has failed at West Hartlepool and has been given assistance forward by locally based Ivatt 2-6-0 No 43128. The sorry ensemble pass Cowpen signalbox, approaching Billingham. *F. S. Gilbert/IAL*

On 8 May 1960 a Sunday engineering diversion between Hitchin and Peterborough sees No 60015 *Quicksilver* restarting the 2.55pm King's Cross to Newcastle train after taking water on the through goods line at Cambridge. *G. D. King/ IAL*

On 17 August 1960 Haymarket's rather grimy No 60011 *Empire of India* is on unfamiliar territory as she passes Symington on the ex-Caledonian route to Carlisle with the 10-coach 10.20am Aberdeen to Euston service. Workings of East Coast Pacifics to Carlisle, apart from during the 1951-3 period, when Polmadie had an allocation of 'A1s', were relatively rare. *K. M. Falconer/IAL*

Sunday 11 September 1960 saw services between Durham and Darlington diverted via Bishop Auckland. Here King's Cross-allocated No 60032 *Gannet* heads for home with the diverted 10.25am Edinburgh to King's Cross service, leaving Bishop Auckland and passing the Spennymoor branch on the right. The former No 4900 had gained her Kylchap exhaust and double chimney in November 1958. *I. S. Carr/IAL*

On Sunday 18 June 1961 the diversions were via the Leamside line between Newcastle and Ferryhill. Here Haymarket's No 60031 *Golden Plover* heads the 10.25am Edinburgh to King's Cross service past Wapping Bridge signalbox, between Penshaw and Fencehouses. At this time the former No 4497 was a regular on the 'Elizabethan' and it is probably the reversed headboard that she is carrying. *I. S. Carr/IAL*

On 27 August 1961 the main line was closed between Relly Mill and Darlington, requiring diversions via Bishop Auckland. This time Haymarket's No 60009 *Union of South Africa* is on the 10.25am service to Kings Cross, heading up the grade away from the main line and towards Dearness Valley signalbox. The lines to the left join at Baxter Wood Junction for Lanchester and Blackhill. *I. S. Carr/IAL*

An early snowfall on 2 December 1961 has covered the fells around Whitrope as Haymarket's No 60031 *Golden Plover* carries Class 2 headlamps while working the 6.40am Waverley to Carlisle local. *W. S. Sellar/IAL*

On 30 June 1962 Gateshead-allocated No 60002 *Sir Murrough Wilson*, in typically grubby Gateshead condition, appears to have been borrowed by Holbeck to cover for one of its 'A3s' for a return trip to Glasgow via the S&C and G&SW routes as she waits to depart from Kilmarnock with the 9.20am Glasgow St Enoch to St Pancras 'Thames Clyde Express' service. *W. G. Sumner/IAL*

Special occasions

Over the years the 'A4s' were involved in many special trains, but none could equal the feat achieved on 23 May 1959. With the imminent retirement of No 60007 *Sir Nigel Gresley*'s regular driver and SLS member Bill Hoole, and the Golden Jubilee of the Stephenson Locomotive Society, the latter arranged the 'Golden Jubilee' special return train from King's Cross to Doncaster, to be hauled by No 60007 and driven by Bill himself. During the day three separate maximum speeds of over 100mph were achieved, with a post-war record maximum descending Stoke of 112mph.

Some years later Bill confided to me that he had carefully studied *Mallard*'s record run and had intended to go for the record. Higher authority intervened when the Civil

At King's Cross station No 60007 *Sir Nigel Gresley* is ready to depart with her regular driver, Bill Hoole, in charge. Today Bill and 'No 7' have illustrious company in the form of author and railway performance recorder O. S. Nock, wearing his characteristic goggles and flat cap. *L. F. Burley/Gresley Society*

Bill Hoole's swansong was the SLS 'Golden Jubilee' special from King's Cross to Doncaster and back on 23 July 1959. Here an immaculate No 60007 *Sir Nigel Gresley*, by now fitted with Kylchap exhaust and double chimney, heads the train north past Holloway. During the day three separate maximum speeds of over 100mph were reached with a post-war record maximum effort of 112mph, recorded for posterity by Peter Handford on his Transacord LP 'Triumph of an A4 Pacific'. *E. R. Wethersett/IAL*

8 June 1961 was a very special day for the 'A4s'. The Duke of Kent was married at York Minster and this required three 'A4'-hauled specials from King's Cross, including the former LNER Royal Train. King's Cross turned out three immaculate 'A4s', Nos 60003 *Andrew K. McCosh* and 60015 *Quicksilver*, and No 60028 *Walter K. Whigham*, with a specially painted white cab roof, for the Royal Train itself. No 60014 *Silver Link* was the stand-by locomotive. The return trains started back from Malton after the reception at Castle Howard, and here No 60028 gets into her stride away from Malton, carrying the correct Royal Train headcode of four headlamps. *O. Hardy/Gresley Society*

As a celebrity locomotive No 60022 *Mallard* was very popular for special trains. On 30 September 1961 one of Alan Pegler's Northern Rubber Company charter trains from Doncaster to Blackpool and back passes Rishton between Accrington and Blackburn. *R. J. Farrell/IAL*

Engineer's specially increased line speed of 110mph was exceeded, and the record attempt came to a frustrating end. So ended another epic performance by an 'A4', almost a quarter of a century after *Silver Link*'s amazing debut in 1935. Although the story of the 'A4s' still had some years to run, there would never be another run like this.

Another very special date in the annals of 'A4' running on the East Coast was on the occasion of the wedding of the Duke of Kent and Katherine Worsley at York Minster on 8 June 1961. In addition to the ex-LNER Royal Train, the number of guests travelling from London required two other 1st Class special trains. After the reception at Castle Howard, all three specials returned from Malton to King's Cross. Despite the fact that diesels, including the new 'Deltics', were by then covering the majority of East Coast expresses, the ER management had insufficient confidence in the reliability of their new diesels to work such high-profile trains and 'A4s' were chosen to haul all three services. King's Cross shed turned out three immaculate locomotives, together with a stand-by, with white cab roofs on Nos 60028 and 60014, and all unpainted metal parts burnished to a very high standard (no silver paint being permitted!) on all four locomotives. The day's events went off without a hitch, all services returning before time despite late starts., including a maximum speed of 100mph down Stoke bank with one of the returning guest specials. Top Shed selected No 60028 *Walter K. Whigham* to work the Royal Train, with Nos 60003 *Andrew K. McCosh* and 60015 *Quicksilver* working the other two specials, and No 60014 *Silver Link* as the stand-by. None of these locomotives was to survive beyond the end of April 1963.

One of the last special 'A4' occasions took place on Saturday 2 March 1962, when the RCTS sponsored 'The Aberdeen Flyer' from King's Cross. The train was advertised as 'the last non-stop steam run of all' between London and Edinburgh, an ambition sadly frustrated by a signal stop at Chathill following a hot box on a preceding freight train. For the London to Edinburgh leg the locomotive selected was the record-breaking No 60022 *Mallard*, the train being worked forward from Edinburgh by No 60004 *William Whitelaw*. To celebrate the 25th anniversary of *Mallard*'s record run, on 7 July 1963 the LCGB ran a special to Doncaster, which, as *Mallard* herself had already been withdrawn, was hauled by No 60007 *Sir Nigel Gresley*. A maximum speed of 103.5mph was achieved descending Stoke bank.

The beginning of the end

On 29 December 1962 the first five 'A4' withdrawals took place (apart from the demise of No 4469 in 1942), with the original No 60014 *Silver Link* being joined by Nos 60028 *Walter K. Whigham*, 60003 *Andrew K. McCosh*, 60033 *Seagull* and 60030 *Golden Fleece*, all withdrawn from Top Shed. No 60014 had run a little over 1.5 million miles during its 27 years in service, and its ignominious fate at Doncaster was an unfitting end for a magnificent machine that for many represented the pinnacle of perfection of British express passenger steam locomotive development. Although no fewer than six 'A4s' have been preserved, including the iconic *Mallard*, the loss of No 2509 is still mourned by many Gresley enthusiasts to this day.

April saw a further three withdrawals from King's Cross, Nos 60015 *Quicksilver*, 60013 *Dominion of New Zealand* and 60022 *Mallard*, the latter fortunately not to share the fate of *Silver Link* and becoming the first 'A4' to be withdrawn for preservation. A few weeks before withdrawal, No 60022 was still sprightly enough to be recorded taking the 11-coach 2.00pm 'Tees-Thames' from King's Cross to Grantham, recovering

On 9 October 1963 No 60021 *Wild Swan* is only 11 days away from being condemned as she enters Sheffield Midland station at the head of the 12.15pm Newcastle to Bristol service. Although based at Peterborough, the former No 4467 is covering a Heaton diagram, which should have terminated at York, so presumably a diesel failure has caused the working to be extended. How far south did the 'A4' get? *R. Tomkin/IAL*

14 minutes of delays and climbing from Essendine to Stoke at an average speed of 80.6mph, and achieving a punctual arrival at Grantham.

With the run-down of steam on the East Coast and the improved reliability of the diesels, the inevitable end of Top Shed at King's Cross came on 16 June 1963, and its 11 surviving 'A4s' were moved to Peterborough New England shed. The distribution of 'A4s' was now New England (11), Gateshead (9), Haymarket (2), St Rollox (2) and Aberdeen

(3). The withdrawal of No 60018 *Sparrow Hawk* from Gateshead on 19 June was quickly followed by the second withdrawal for preservation, when No 60008 *Dwight D. Eisenhower* was withdrawn from New England on 20 July.

With the end of the 1963 summer services there was little work left for the 'A4s'. The last recorded normal working of an 'A4' from King's Cross was undertaken by New England's No 60017 *Silver Fox*, which worked the 6.40pm Leeds express on 19 October.

On a fine spring day in 1962, No 60022 *Mallard* has only a year's service left as, with safety valves just lifting, she prepares to leave Grantham with an up Leeds and Bradford to King's Cross express. Note the commemorative plaque fitted to the boiler-side in 1947 recording her World Record achieved in 1938. *C. J. B. Sanderson/ Colour-Rail BRE 688*

Shortly afterwards this locomotive and four others, Nos 60021 *Wild Swan*, 60025 *Falcon*, 60029 *Woodcock* and 60032 *Gannet*, were all withdrawn from New England.

The five survivors (Nos 60006/07/10/26/34) were then transferred to Scotland, together with four from Gateshead (Nos 60005/16/19/23). The finale at King's Cross was on 24 October 1964 when the RCTS/SLS 'Jubilee Requiem' special was worked by Ferryhill-allocated No 60009 *Union of South Africa* to Newcastle and back. On the return journey the maximum speed down Stoke bank was 96mph and arrival at King's Cross was 26 minutes early, having kept well ahead of the following diesel-hauled Leeds express from Peterborough. The three surviving 'A4s' at Gateshead only survived to 20 March (No 60020), 5 April (No 60002) and finally No 60001 *Sir Ronald Matthews* on 12 October. No 60001 was unusual in only ever having been allocated to Gateshead shed throughout its 26 years of service.

June 1962 was rather late in the day to be able to catch two 'A4s' passing each other. No 60010 *Dominion of Canada* impatiently blows off as she waits to start an up express and is passed by No 60013 *Dominion of New Zealand* hauling train No 266 Down, the afternoon King's Cross Scotch Goods, which was for many years a King's Cross top link job.
D. W. Webb/Colour-Rail BRE 839

On a cold and frosty January morning in 1963 No 60029 *Woodcock* is only nine months away from withdrawal as she puts on a really atmospheric display climbing Holloway bank with a down express. The former No 4493 was among the last ten 'A4s' to be based at King's Cross at closure on 16 June 1963.
J. F. Aylard/Colour-Rail BRE 923

In January 1963 No 60007 *Sir Nigel Gresley* brings an up parcels train through a snowy Potters Bar. Despite being only six months away from closure, King's Cross shed is apparently still keeping its last 'A4s' in excellent external condition, although No 60007 was a railtour favourite, so could have received special attention.
A. J. Reeve/Colour-Rail BRE 2004

CHAPTER SEVEN

THE SCOTTISH FINALE

The deployment of 'A4s' within Scotland had been traditionally confined to services over former LNER routes between Edinburgh and Aberdeen, Perth via Glenfarg, and Glasgow Queen Street. Traditionally, since the allocation of brand-new No 4483 *Kingfisher* in December 1936, Haymarket shed had housed the entire Scottish allocation of 'A4s'. In 1949, No 60012 *Commonwealth of Australia* spent some months on loan to Polmadie, working on the West Coast Main Line to Carlisle, but the allocation of Nos 60031 *Golden Plover* and 60027 *Merlin* to the former Caledonian shed at Balornock (St Rollox) in February and May 1962 respectively was the beginning of the deployment of the class on the internal services between Glasgow Buchanan Street and both Aberdeen and Dundee. No 60027, still allocated to Haymarket at the time, was used to work a return test run between Buchanan Street and Aberdeen on 22 February 1962 in order to validate the accelerated timings required to achieve overall 3-hour timings on this route. Also in May and June respectively, Nos 60009 *Union of South Africa* and 60004 *William Whitelaw* moved from Haymarket to Ferryhill shed at Aberdeen, again the first 'A4s' to be allocated to this shed, although visits by Haymarket locomotives on workings from Edinburgh had been common since 1937.

The LMS had progressively improved the Glasgow to Aberdeen service during the 1930s, culminating in the first 3-hour services in 1937, hauled by 'Jubilee' class 4-6-0s. The new eight-coach 'St Mungo' and 'Bon Accord' trains supplemented the long-standing ex-Caledonian 'Granite City' and 'Grampian Corridor' services. In the summer of 1956 the majority of intermediate stations between Perth and Aberdeen (via Forfar) were closed to passenger traffic and the entire express train service between Glasgow and both Aberdeen and Dundee was put on an even-interval basis with accelerated overall schedules of 3hr 30min. This service was worked reasonably successfully by both

On a frosty 2 March 1963 Haymarket's No 60012 *Commonwealth of Australia* races down the 1 in 100 gradient through Bridge of Allan with the 1.30pm Aberdeen to Glasgow 'Grampian' towards its stop at Stirling. The use of 'A4s' (and some 'A3s') on the Glasgow to Aberdeen 3-hour expresses had begun with the summer timetable of 1962, boosted by the arrival of nine former English 'A4s' in the summer of 1964. *Derek Cross/IAL*

In May 1964 Ferryhill-based No 60009 *Union of South Africa* heads the 5.30pm Glasgow Buchanan Street to Aberdeen 'Bon Accord' near Luncarty, just north of Perth on the now abandoned Caledonian main line through Forfar to Kinnaber Junction. *W. J. V. Anderson/IAL*

Steam/diesel combinations were not uncommon in the 1960s. On 6 July 1964 Ferryhill's No 60004 *William Whitelaw* (29 years of service) is assisted into Perth by Eastfield-allocated NB/MAN Type 2 diesel No D6118 (nine years in traffic) with the 2.11pm fish service from Aberdeen to Carlisle. The headcode marker discs on the diesel are obviously not in use as otherwise they indicate a Royal Train! *D. C. Smith/IAL*

ex-LMS and BR Standard Class 5 locomotives. From 1959 onwards some of the Type 4 2,000hp diesels began to be used on filling-in duties between use on both the East and West Coast routes, but the first diesel types to be allocated to the Scottish Region were the North British 1,000hp and BRCW 1,160hp Type 2 Bo-Bos, later to be joined at Inverness by an allocation of Derby/Sulzer 1,160hp Bo-Bos.

The Scottish Region's aspiration to make full use of these new locomotives was quickly frustrated by their unreliability, so the desire to accelerate services would either have to be postponed or, of necessity, be achieved by steam. The Scottish Region had decided on a policy of elimination of steam, area by area, and by 1962 had almost completed dieselisation of the Highlands and West Highland lines, so Glasgow to Aberdeen was a lower priority. The region was fortunate to be blessed with a visionary

On a clear summer evening in July 1964, and with Edinburgh clearly visible in the distance across the Firth of Forth, Ferryhill-based No 60006 *Sir Ralph Wedgwood* heads for home with the 6.15pm Millerhill to Aberdeen Craiginches freight, largely conveying empty 'Blue Spot' fish vans, near Kinghorn in Fife. *W. J. V. Anderson/IAL*

On 29 August 1964 Ferryhill-based No 60007 *Sir Nigel Gresley* emerges from Buchanan Street tunnel climbing the 1 in 79 gradient with the 5.30pm Buchanan Street to Aberdeen 'St Mungo' express. *S. Rickard/IAL*

General Manager, James Ness, and it was apparently he who suggested the use of 'A4s' to work the Glasgow to Aberdeen services, which, from the summer 1962 timetable, were to be accelerated to restore the pre-war 3-hour schedules. Initially the 'A4s' were welcomed by the Aberdeen and Perth crews, who were familiar with the class, but at Balornock the ex-LMS crews were more reluctant. However, when a threat to re-diagram the work away to other sheds was made, they fell into line and the 'A4s' settled down to almost four years of solid work.

In 1964, Ferryhill's No 60006 *Sir Ralph Wedgwood* comes off the Forth Bridge and through South Queensferry station with an Aberdeen to Edinburgh express. *A4 Locomotive Society*

In April 1965 the 10.15 Ditton Junction to Bathgate 20-carflat train of new Ford cars has been provided with 'super power' while leaving Carlisle against the 1 in 75 gradients of the 'Waverley' route. Train engine No 60024 *Kingfisher* of Ferryhill is assisted by locally based 'Black Five' No 44672. *Peter J. Robinson/IAL*

Typically the locomotives soon showed that the 19-minute allowance over the 16 hilly miles from Aberdeen to Stonehaven, which even the 2,000hp Type 4 diesels struggled to achieve and was impossible with the Type 2s, was habitually reduced to 17½ minutes by the 'A4s'. In addition to the Glasgow to Aberdeen expresses the 'A4s' found

A regular ex-LNER Pacific turn until 1966 was the 15.30 Aberdeen to Euston 'West Coast Postal', more properly the 'North Western Night Up Special TPO', which was worked from Aberdeen through to Carstairs. Having dropped the passenger portion at Perth but still carrying Class 1 headlamps, Ferryhill's No 60006 *Sir Ralph Wedgwood* departs from Stirling on 21 April 1965. *J. S. Whiteley/IAL*

regular work between Aberdeen and Carstairs hauling the famous 'West Coast Postal' service, which actually ran as a passenger train as far south as Perth. They continued to be used between Aberdeen and Edinburgh, particularly on reliefs, specials and weekend services when the regular diesels were frequently unavailable, receiving much-needed servicing and repairs!

By January 1963 Ferryhill had swapped No 60004 for No 60011 *Empire of India* from Haymarket, leaving the same two 'A4s' (Nos 60027/31) at St Rollox, three at Haymarket (Nos 60004/12/24) and two at Ferryhill (Nos 60009/11). Of the nine 'A4s' transferred to the Scottish Region in October 1963, seven, nominally all allocated to St Margarets shed, were initially placed into store — Nos 60006/7 at Dalry Road, 60016/19 at Ferryhill, 60023 at Bathgate and 60026/34 at Galashiels — for only a month before joining No 60023 at Bathgate. No 60005 *Sir Charles Newton* stayed for two weeks at St Margarets before moving to Ferryhill, while No 60010 *Dominion of Canada* went straight to Ferryhill. The Scottish Region had already stored Nos 60012 and 60024 at Dalry Road on the closure of Haymarket shed on 9 September 1963, and at the start of October had only five active 'A4s', Nos 60004/09/11 at Ferryhill and 60027/31 at Balornock (St Rollox). The Region took a few weeks to assess the condition of its newly

With the Tay Bridge in the background on a fine 21 June 1965, Ferryhill's No 60007 *Sir Nigel Gresley* has plenty of steam to spare as it accelerates the 14-van pigeon special empties, returning to King's Cross from Aberdeen past Wormit signalbox. The former No 4498 had emerged from the last of its three works visits to Inverurie on 11 April 1965, one of eight 'A4s' to visit this ex-GNoS facility during 1965/6. *Paul Riley/IAL*

acquired assets, and by the 1964 summer timetable all were back in active service, except Nos 60005 (withdrawn on 12 March 1964) and 60011 (withdrawn on 11 May 1964), giving in June a total of 14 active 'A4s', ten at Ferryhill, two at St Rollox and two at St Margarets. Further 1964 withdrawals, both from Ferryhill, were No 60012 *Commonwealth of Australia* on 20 August and No 60023 *Golden Eagle* on 30 October. By January 1965 the situation was only 11 active, with eight at Ferryhill

(Nos 60004/06/07/09/10/19/26/34), two at St Margarets (Nos 60024/27) and only No 60031 at Balornock.(No 60027 having moved to St Margarets at the end of the summer timetable in September 1964).

A further six withdrawals took place in 1965, all but No 60027 from Ferryhill shed. No 60016 was withdrawn in March, 60010 in May, 60006 and 60027 (from St Margarets) at the end of the summer timetable in September, followed by Nos 60031

In early July 1965 St Rollox-based No 60031 *Golden Plover* departs from Dundee with the 09.30 Aberdeen to Edinburgh express. The departure is being observed from above by the crew of locally based 'J37' 0-6-0 No 64558, engaged in shunting the goods yard. Note that the former No 4497 has now acquired a yellow stripe on her cabside, indicating a ban on working under the overhead electric lines south of Crewe. This locomotive had her last works visit, to Cowlairs, from 21 July to 7 August before being condemned on 29 October 1965. *J. R. P. Hunt/IAL*

in October and 60026 in December, leaving a final six locomotives in service, all based at Ferryhill, at the end of that year. The next two withdrawals were much more fortunate, with No 60007 *Sir Nigel Gresley* being withdrawn for preservation on 1 February and No 60009 *Union of South Africa* similarly on 1 June. For the summer timetable of 1966, this left four active locomotives for three diagrams. The next locomotives to expire were No 60004 *William Whitelaw* on 17 July and the last-built and 1948 Locomotive Exchange celebrity No 60034 *Lord Faringdon* on 24 August. On Saturday 3 September the Scottish Region took the opportunity to run a special final 3-hour steam-hauled express from Glasgow to Aberdeen and back, worked by No 60019 *Bittern*. With the end of the 1966 summer timetable the last two survivors, *Bittern* and No 60024 *Kingfisher*, were finally withdrawn on Monday 5 September, bringing to an end 29 years of illustrious service.

On 7 July 1965 Ferryhill's No 60007 *Sir Nigel Gresley* makes a stirring sight accelerating away from Aberdeen under a fine ex-Caledonian signal gantry with the 13.30 Aberdeen to Buchanan Street 'Grampian' express. *Maurice Burns/IAL*

On 24 July 1965 another Ferryhill 'A4', No 60009 *Union of South Africa*, gets into her stride through Princes Street Gardens as she leaves Waverley station with a troop special for Aberdeen.
Paul Riley/IAL

On 31 July 1965 a rather grimy St Margarets-allocated No 60027 *Merlin* has plenty of steam to spare as she heads for home away from Dundee Tay Bridge station with the 09.10 Aberdeen to Edinburgh express. The former No 4486 survived for only another five weeks, until 3 September 1965. Note the cabside yellow stripe.
D. Mackinnon/IAL

On a frosty November afternoon in 1965, Ferryhill's No 60026 *Miles Beevor* has had a recent clean as she storms out of Aberdeen with the 13.30 express to Glasgow, the 'Grampian'. Withdrawn on 21 December, the following year the former No 4485 *Kestrel* was used as a source of spare parts for the restoration of No 4498 *Sir Nigel Gresley* at Crewe, so at least her driving wheel sets survived.
Dougald Cameron/IAL

During a blizzard on 19 February 1966 Ferryhill's No 60019 *Bittern* makes a smoky departure from Gleneagles with the 'Grampian' express. The former No 4464 was one of the last two 'A4s' to survive in normal service, being withdrawn for preservation on 5 September 1966. *Paul Riley/IAL*

By 9 April 1966 the weather had improved, as Ferryhill's No 60024 *Kingfisher* leaves a plume of exhaust over Gleneagles as she departs with the 'Grampian'. The former No 4483 was the other final surviving 'A4', but suffered a less happy fate, being scrapped at Blyth in October 1966. *W. Alexander/IAL*

There was to be a further surprising final fling as, a week later on Tuesday 13 September, No 60024 *Kingfisher* was resurrected by Ferryhill to work the 17.15 Aberdeen to Glasgow 'Granite City', returning on the morning of the 14th with the 08.25 Buchanan Street to Aberdeen express. Absolutely the last normal BR service to be 'A4'-hauled was a Perth-Aberdeen-Edinburgh special on Easter Saturday, 25 March 1967, when No 60009 *Union of South Africa*, assisted by 'Black Five' No 44997, hauled an 18-coach 640-ton special throughout, including finally taking the empty stock from Waverley to Craigentinny unassisted.

On 14 April 1966 No 60034 *Lord Faringdon*, another Ferryhill locomotive, approaches Cumbernauld with the 13.30 Aberdeen to Glasgow 'Grampian' express. The former No 4903 *Peregrine* survived only until 24 August 1966, sharing a similar fate to No 60024. *Paul Riley/IAL*

On 30 May 1966 Ferryhill's No 60019 *Bittern* blows off furiously as she approaches Carmont on the 1 in 102 climb out of Stonehaven with the 17.15 Aberdeen to Glasgow 'Granite City' express. *Paul Riley/IAL*

Two days before withdrawal, on 3 September 1966, Ferryhill's No 60019 *Bittern* climbs the 1 in 79 St Rollox bank with an 09.55 BR special to Aberdeen and back to commemorate the last 'A4'-hauled 3-hour Aberdeen express.
Trevor Rees/IAL

In 1962 No 60006 *Sir Ralph Wedgwood* roars through Gleneagles station with a long Aberdeen to London express, diverted via Stirling because of engineering works on the Forth Bridge. The former No 4466 was named *Herring Gull* between 1938 and 1944 when she was renamed after the LNER Chief General Manager. *J. M. Cramp/Colour-Rail SC 1467*

In May 1964
No 60009 *Union of
South Africa* waits to
depart from Stirling
with the 7.10am
Aberdeen to Glasgow
Buchanan Street
express. The former
No 4488 began her
first two months of
service as *Osprey* until
becoming the first
Garter blue 'A4' and
being renamed on
28 June 1937.
No 60009, in BR days
always known as
simply 'No 9', was
always a Scottish
engine, being allocated
to Haymarket until
May 1962 when a final
move for her last 3½
years took her to
Aberdeen. Always a
celebrity, on 6
November 1963,
'No 9' was the last
steam engine to have
a normal repair at
Doncaster Works, and
on 24 October 1964
she was the last 'A4' to
work a normal service
train out of King's
Cross. She is one of
the six 'A4s' to be
preserved.
*M. Smith/Colour-Rail
SC 1280*

In June 1964
Aberdeen-allocated
No 60012
*Commonwealth of
Australia* heads the
well-loaded 6.15pm
Millerhill to
Craiginches
(Aberdeen) Class 4
freight past Blackford
Hill signalbox on the
Edinburgh South
Suburban line. The
former No 4491 was
always a Scottish 'A4',
having active
allocations at only
Haymarket and
Aberdeen, separated
by five months in store
at Dalry Road after
unclassified repairs at
Inverurie in
September 1963.
No 60012 had to wait
until July 1958 before
acquiring her double
chimney.
*George M. Staddon/
Colour-Rail SC 897*

In April 1965, No 60031 *Golden Plover* makes a relatively rare 'A4' venture over the 'Waverley' route and is seen here just south of the line's summit at Whitrope, leaving Riccarton Junction station with an up special train. The former No 4497 was another exclusively Scottish 'A4', being allocated for 24 years to Haymarket, with a final 3 years 8 months at the former Caledonian Railway's St Rollox shed in Glasgow. *A. E. R. Cope/ Colour-Rail SC 207*

Earlier in the same journey, and 33 miles further north along the 'Waverley' route, No 60031 rests at Galashiels. Note the break on the streamlined casing to provide access to the mechanical lubricators and the diagonal yellow stripe added in the mid-1960s to indicate that the 'A4s' were too high to be allowed to work under the newly energised 25kv overhead line equipment on the West Coast Main Line south of Crewe – not natural territory for an 'A4'! *R. Biddick/ Colour-Rail SC 1468*

In July 1965 the last-built 'A4', No 60034 *Lord Faringdon*, comes off the Forth Bridge at North Queensferry with a long Millerhill to Aberdeen Class 4 freight. The former No 4903, which always carried a double chimney, was based at Aberdeen for its last two years of service. The semaphore junction signal guarding the up line is for the bi-directional signalling over the Forth Bridge.
Colour-Rail SC 4

Two months later, in September 1965, *Lord Faringdon* is still active although now only just over a year from withdrawal as she drifts down the 1 in 100 gradient through Bridge of Allan towards the Stirling stop with the six-coach 06.20 Aberdeen to Glasgow Buchanan Street 'Bon Accord' express. The former No 4903 *Peregrine* acquired the name of the former LNER Deputy Chairman in March 1948, after the GCR 4-6-0 that formerly carried his name had just been scrapped. No 60034 was a long-term King's Cross resident before moving to St Margarets and Aberdeen for her last three years in traffic. *J. W. Millbank/ Colour-Rail SC 1170*

In May 1966,
No 60019 *Bittern* gets
to grips with the 1½
miles of 1 in 79 as she
departs from Glasgow
Buchanan Street
station with the 08.25
express to Aberdeen.
The former No 4464
was a long-term
Heaton and
Gateshead resident
until transfer to
Scotland in October
1963, briefly to
St Margarets, and
finally in November
1963, for her last
three years of regular
service, to Aberdeen.
No 60019 was one of
the last two 'A4s' to
be withdrawn, in
September 1966,
before being
purchased for
preservation. In late
2007 it has rejoined
the exclusive list of
main-line-registered
'A4s'. *S. M. Watkins/
Colour-Rail SC 1138*

'A4 finale': in the autumn of 1966, No 60024 *Kingfisher* is less than a week away from withdrawal on 5 September as her driver carries out his preparation duties while she rests on the turntable at the very cramped St Margarets shed in Edinburgh. By this time Haymarket was a diesel depot and any visiting Aberdeen-based 'A4s' had to be serviced at St Margarets. This is an excellent view of an 'A4' in her final condition with electrification warning flashes visible about the locomotive. The former No 4483 *Kingfisher* was one of the last two 'A4s' in service, but did not survive into preservation, being scrapped at Hughes Bolckow, Blyth, in October 1966. The non-corridor tender, No 5640, had only been attached for her last two weeks of service, being acquired from No 60034 on that locomotive's withdrawal at Aberdeen on 24 August and replacing corridor tender No 5329, which had presumably become defective.
George M. Staddon/Colour-Rail SC 898

CHAPTER EIGHT

PRESERVATION

No 4468/60022 *Mallard*

No 60022 *Mallard* had been earmarked for preservation in 1960 and, on a visit to Doncaster for classified repairs in April 1963, was found to be beyond the limits then set for repair costs. Withdrawal came on 25 April 1963 and No 4468 thus became the first 'A4' to be preserved. Doncaster undertook what was supposed to be a cosmetic restoration, but when the locomotive was being considered for restoration to working order in 1986 it was discovered that Doncaster had in fact done a very thorough job, without which the 1986 return to steam would have been impossibly expensive. On withdrawal No 60022 was coupled to corridor tender No 5651, whereas on 3 July 1938 she ran with non-corridor tender No 5642. By 1963 this tender was attached to

No 60026 *Miles Beevor*, still very much in active service operating from King's Cross. Non-corridor tender No 5670 from recently scrapped No 60003 *Andrew K. McCosh* was thus used, being renumbered No 5642 to suit. As the original No 5642 survived beyond the withdrawal of No 60026 in 1965, to be eventually scrapped in Leeds in 1973, for at least ten years there were two 'A4' tenders both numbered 5642!

No 4468 was earmarked for display in the new British Transport Museum located in a non-rail-connected former bus garage at Clapham in South London. Restoration having been completed by February 1964, the locomotive was hauled by rail from Doncaster to Nine Elms Goods Yard via the Great Central main line through Nottingham Victoria on 26 February. Then, on 29 February, with engine and tender

The first of the six 'A4s' to be preserved was No 60022 *Mallard*. Earmarked for preservation in 1960, on arrival at Doncaster works in 1963 the former No 4468 was found to be beyond economic repair and was thus condemned on 25 April and withdrawn for preservation. Doncaster did a thorough restoration back to 1938 condition. By February 1964 the loco was ready to be placed in the then British Transport Museum at Clapham. Here, at 10.00pm on 29 February 1964, No 4468 is stuck across Nine Elms Lane after the leading bogie of the low-loader sank into the pavement and became stuck fast for several hours, completely blocking the road. *Brian Stephenson/IAL*

After the closure of Clapham, in 1975 No 4468 was moved to the new National Railway Museum at York. In anticipation of the 50th anniversary of her World Record run, No 4468 was restored to full working order on a restricted boiler ticket permitting a maximum of 26 runs. The first public run was to Scarborough on 9 July 1986 and here she makes an impressively smoky departure from York past a crowd of admirers. *Brian Dobbs/ IAL*

On 4 October 1986 No 4468 was used to haul the 'South Yorkshire Pullman' from York to Marylebone via Derby and Banbury. Here *Mallard* heads the train, formed of the SLOA Pullman set, out of Milford Tunnel between Belper and Derby. The move south was to position the locomotive for a series of 'Shakespeare Express' trains.
R. P. Middleton/IAL

On Saturday 8 November 1986, No 4468 *Mallard* worked the SLOA Pullman set back from Marylebone to York with the 'Peter Allen Pullman', pictured here passing Kilnhurst, just north of Rotherham.
J. S. Whiteley/IAL

The second trip to Stratford-upon-Avon was on 26 October 1986 and here a gleaming No 4468 heads the return working to Marylebone up the 1 in 75 gradient towards Wilmcote.
Peter Tandy/IAL

The third 'Shakespeare Express was on 2 November, and on that cool winter morning *Mallard* provides a spectacular exhaust display as she gets her train away from Marylebone station.
J. H. Cooper-Smith/IAL

separated, the move was made by road low-loader to the museum. With the decision to create a National Railway Museum at York, the Clapham Museum closed in 1975 and No 4468 moved north from Stewarts Lane to York on 12 April 1975.

With the approach of the 50th Anniversary of *Mallard*'s World Record run on 3 July 1988, attention focused on the possibility of No 4468 appearing again in steam. With

The next main-line outing for No 4468 was to celebrate the 10th Anniversary of the NRM on 25 and 26 April 1987, when a York-Harrogate-Leeds-York-Scarborough and return itinerary was worked throughout by No 4468. On the Sunday morning, 26 April, the locomotive leans to the curve at Clifton Bridge past York Yard North with the run to Harrogate and Leeds.
W. A. Sharman/IAL

On the 50th anniversary of her World Record run on 3 July 1988, No 4468 *Mallard* worked a Doncaster to York and return special, the first East Coast Main Line steam since 1964 apart from specials hauled by No 4472. Before departing from Doncaster one generation of East Coast greyhound stands alongside another as No 4468 poses alongside an ex-works Class 91 electric locomotive.
Peter Harris/IAL

the NRM operating on a strictly limited budget, Scarborough Borough Council generously agreed to sponsor the overhaul, and this was advanced to 1986 in order to earn as much income as possible from the operation of the locomotive. As the restoration budget only covered a partial overhaul, the main line 'ticket' was issued on a restricted basis, limited to a maximum of 26 runs over five years. *Mallard* was steamed for the first time in 22 years on the occasion of the 10th Anniversary celebrations at the NRM on 27 September 1985.

By 25 March 1986, No 4468 was ready to move under her own steam on a single-coach test train via Scarborough and Hull to Doncaster Works, where final weighing and adjustments were made, including a final application of new Garter blue paint. The first passenger run was on the inaugural 'Scarborough Spa Express' on 9 July 1986. Other workings of this train were hauled by No 5305 and No 3440 *City of Truro*, with No 4468 making a second appearance on 25 August when the train had to be

After an over-subscribed series of ten 'Mallard 88' Scarborough trips, on 27 August 1988 No 4468 worked her last main-line trip, a circular Eaglescliffe-Newcastle-Carlisle-Leeds-York special. Unfortunately the southbound climb over the Settle & Carlisle line to Ais Gill left No 4468 a little winded and here she coasts to a stop for a 'blow-up' at Birkett Common, just short of Ais Gill summit.
Dr L. A. Nixon/IAL

strengthened to 13 coaches, such was the demand. A further one-way trip from York to Scarborough took place on 4 September as part of a cricket festival sponsored by Asda. An invitation to visit the French National Railway Museum at Mulhouse for its 10th Anniversary celebrations on 27 and 28 September 1986 was accepted and, in return for free shipment to France, it was agreed that No 4468 would work several of the BR-sponsored 'Shakespeare Limited' trains between Marylebone and Stratford-upon-Avon. The visit to Mulhouse did not take place, but No 4468 worked south to Marylebone on 4 October with the 'South Yorkshire Pullman'. Three 'Shakespeare Limited' trains to Stratford-upon-Avon were worked on 12 and 26 October, and on 2 November, with No 4468 returning to York at the head of the 'Peter Allan Pullman' on 8 November. *Mallard* then retired to the NRM for a well-earned rest before the planned celebrations in 1988.

The 10th Anniversary of the Friends of the National Railway Museum took place on 25 April 1987 and to celebrate No 4468 reappeared on a 'Scarborough Spa' itinerary,

repeated owing to popular demand on the 26th. An RSPB-sponsored special from York to Carnforth followed on 16 May, with a York-Manchester return trip on 25 May. For the Doncaster Works Open Day on 3 October 1987 No 4468, together with No 92220 *Evening Star*, was worked from York to Doncaster and back. Thus, in 1987, No 4468 worked four trains and two light movements.

1988 was to be the year of the big event, to be celebrated by the Post Office with a special release of commemorative stamps. This began with a press launch and test run with Travelling Post Office (TPO) vehicles travelling York-Harrogate-Leeds-York on 6 May before working the Post Office exhibition train to Marylebone for two days of display on 8 and 9 May. On the 9th a 'Postal Pullman' special was worked to Banbury followed the next day by the 'Pennine Postal Pullman' from Manchester to Scarborough. On the day of the Anniversary, 3 July, No 4468 took over a London to Scarborough special at Doncaster. The next task was a series of ten 'Scarborough Spa Express' trips, all of which were sold out, in the middle of which were trips on 16 July to Carlisle and on 23 July to Grange-over-Sands. On 30 July No 4468 worked the 'Transpennine' to Manchester for the RCTS, and on 13 and 27 August further trips to Carlisle were worked. That on the 27th was the last main-line trip for No 4468 and was marred by a stop for a 'blow-up' on the return climb to Ais Gill summit on the Settle & Carlisle line, the loco being short of steam due to a blocked spark arrestor. No 4468 then retired to the NRM with her boiler ticket expired, and has only appeared 'dead' at other events such as Doncaster Works Open Days in 1988, 1998 and 2003, together with the 'NRM on Tour' exhibition at Swindon in 1990. Given the current financial situation and the huge expenditure lavished on No 4472 *Flying Scotsman*, No 4468 appears to be somewhat overshadowed at the NRM and a future return to steam seems unlikely.

No 4496/60008 *Golden Shuttle/Dwight D. Eisenhower*

The second 'A4' to be preserved was the former No 4496 *Golden Shuttle*. On 25 September 1945 the locomotive was renamed *Dwight D. Eisenhower* after the Allied Forces Supreme Commander, and was renumbered No 8 on 23 November 1946, and finally 60008 on 29 October 1948.

Always an English-allocated 'A4', No 60008 was the 11th 'A4' to be withdrawn, on 20 July 1963. This time Doncaster only gave a cosmetic restoration of the locomotive in final BR condition, complete with electrification warning flashes (subsequently painted over), AWS equipment and a Smith-Stone speedometer. On 27 April 1964 Dr Beeching, Chairman of the BRB, formally handed over the locomotive at Southampton Docks for shipment by the United States Lines vessel *American Planter*. In a nice touch the locomotive had been hauled from Eastleigh to Southampton Docks by Bulleid 'Merchant Navy' class locomotive No 35012 *United States Lines*. From Chicago the locomotive was moved by rail to the US National Railroad Museum at Green Bay, Wisconsin, where it resides to this day, apparently a little forlorn and uncared for.

No 4489/60010 *Woodcock/Dominion of Canada*

Early in May 1965 the Scottish Region sent No 60010 *Dominion of Canada* from Ferryhill shed to Darlington Works for an Intermediate Heavy repair. The poor condition of the boiler caused the locomotive to be condemned on 29 May, but instead of being offered

On 27 April 1964 No 60008 *Dwight D. Eisenhower* was handed over by BRB Chairman Dr Beeching outside the United States Lines quayside offices in Southampton. United States Lines sponsored the shipment from Southampton to Chicago aboard the *American Planter*. *G. Wheeler/IAL*

After arrival in Chicago, No 60008 is pictured in front of a US Co-Co diesel, prior to movement by rail to the National Railroad Museum at Green Bay, Wisconsin, where she remains to this day. */IAL*

The second 'A4' to be preserved was No 60008 *Dwight D. Eisenhower*. On withdrawal from service on 20 July 1963 the former No 4496 *Golden Shuttle* was given a cosmetic restoration at Doncaster in its final condition. On 22 April 1964 the locomotive was appropriately hauled to Southampton Docks from Eastleigh by No 35012 *United States Lines* and here checks are being made on the curve to the dockside. *G. Wheeler/IAL*

for sale to scrap merchants, it was towed to the running shed at Bank Top. There it remained in a forlorn state for more than a year until August 1966, when it was hauled to Crewe Works to be given, at a cost of £1,600, a cosmetic restoration in its final BR condition.

On 10 April 1967 No 60010 was presented to the Canadian High Commissioner by BRB Member John Ratter aboard the Canadian Pacific freighter *Beaveroak*, moored in

Royal Victoria Dock, London. After shipment to Montreal, No 60010 was moved to the Canadian Railroad Historical Association Museum at Delson near Montreal. The CPR bell, which the loco had carried from 1938 to 1957 until the double chimney conversion required its removal, was returned with the locomotive but not, for obvious reasons, fitted.

No 4498/60007 *Sir Nigel Gresley*

The fourth 'A4' to enter preservation was the famous 100th Gresley Pacific, *Sir Nigel Gresley*. The A4 Preservation Society had launched an appeal for funds in 1965 and this was so successful that in May 1966 it was able both to acquire the locomotive, withdrawn on 1 February 1966, and fund a General Overhaul and restoration to main-line running order at Crewe Works. This commenced in July and, in order to speed the restoration, the most recently withdrawn 'A4', No 60026 *Miles Beevor*, taken out of service on 21 December 1965 at Perth and sold for scrap, was fortuitously recovered from the scrapyard, and by 25 September 1966 was at Crewe Works in order to donate parts. In fact, all of No 60026's driving wheels had better tyres and were transferred to No 4498, to which number 60007 had reverted. Curiously No 60026 also had the original non-corridor tender coupled to No 4468 *Mallard* on 3 July 1938, which came into the ownership of the A4 Society. After several years, including donating some parts to the restoration of No 4472 at Hunslet in Leeds, this tender was surplus to requirements and was scrapped. The restoration of No 4498 was a compromise as the locomotive had acquired a double Kylchap exhaust in December 1957, lost the side skirting in 1942 and had other details changed from the original locomotive as delivered in 1937. The chosen livery was Garter blue with shaded numbers and lettering as originally delivered. The 1939 embellishments of stainless steel cut-out letters and numbers were restored in 1975 prior to the Shildon exhibition

After some running-in trips in March 1967, No 4498 re-entered main-line service with a Crewe to Carlisle return trip on 1 April, out via Shap and back via the S&C and Blackburn. No 4498 was immediately popular traction for a succession of enthusiasts' specials, including a return trip from Edinburgh to Aberdeen on 20 May. This required a positioning move to Scotland, so No 4498 was used to haul several parcels and mails

The third 'A4' to enter preservation was No 60010 *Dominion of Canada*. Early in May 1965 the Scottish Region had sent the former No 4489 *Woodcock* to Darlington for repairs, but the condition of the boiler caused withdrawal on the 29th and she stood forlornly at Darlington until August 1966, when movement to Crewe took place for cosmetic restoration. On 10 April 1967 No 60010 was presented to the Canadian High Commissioner by BRB member John Ratter aboard the Canadian Pacific freighter *Beaveroak* moored in Royal Victoria Dock, London. Here the Port of London Authority floating crane *Mammoth* positions the locomotive as deck cargo. After shipment to Montreal, No 60010 was moved to the Canadian Railroad Historical Association Museum at Delson near Montreal. The CPR bell, which the locomotive carried from 1938 to 1957, was returned with the locomotive but not fitted. *BRE/IAL*

The fourth preserved 'A4' was No 60007 *Sir Nigel Gresley*. The A4 Preservation Society had raised sufficient funds by May 1966 to both acquire the locomotive and pay for restoration to full main-line working order at Crewe works, in part using items from No 60026 *Miles Beevor* to speed the process. The first passenger trip was on 1 April 1966 from Crewe to Carlisle, out via Shap and returning via the S&C and Blackburn. No 4498, restored to LNER Garter blue livery, gives a burst on that lovely chime whistle while heading the southbound special through Dent.
A4 Locomotive Society

In order to position the locomotive for a May special from Edinburgh, No 4498 *Sir Nigel Gresley* was used to haul parcels trains north and here clears Beattock summit hauling 3S06, the Carlisle to Perth parcels, on 17 May 1967. *Derek Cross/IAL*

services over the West Coast route from Crewe to Edinburgh. By June a move to the south of England was made in order to work several specials out of Waterloo station. Before the return north was effected on 23 July an emotional return to King's Cross was made in order to work a trip to Newcastle and back. By 28 October, No 4498 was back on the West Coast racing ground hauling 'The Border Limited' from Crewe to Carlisle.

By now nicely run-in, No 4498 was given the opportunity to show the opposition what a real greyhound could achieve. O. S. Nock recorded the run and commented, 'The start out of Crewe was virtually up to electric standards, for in just 10 minutes from the dead start No 4498 was travelling at 96mph!' The 31.4 miles from Carnforth to Shap

By June 1967 *Sir Nigel Gresley* was in London for a Waterloo to Bournemouth special, repeated the following day throughout to Weymouth. On Saturday 3 June, No 4498 sets out from Waterloo for Bournemouth, past an Ivatt Class 2 2-6-2T on station pilot duties.
B. H. Jackson/IAL

By July, No 4498 was back on East Coast metals, working from King's Cross to Newcastle and back. On the 23rd, the locomotive heads the return train near Croft Spa, south of Darlington.
John Hunt/IAL

summit were covered in three seconds under the half-hour, an average of all but 63mph over a stretch on which the adverse gradient averages 1 in 187. By November the locomotive began losing work as the infamous BR 'steam ban' began to bite, and the locomotive required a new home closer to the mainly North East homes of the support crew. The NCB offered a temporary home at its Philadelphia workshops near Washington, Tyne & Wear, and the locomotive moved from Crewe via Shap, Carlisle and Newcastle on 31 July 1968. With the ending of the steam ban in 1972, No 4498 returned to the main line on 17 June with the 'Steam Safari' railtour from Newcastle to Carlisle and back. Further trips followed in 1973, 1974 and 1975 culminating in an appearance at the S&D 150 celebrations at Shildon on 31 August 1975.

With the expiry of her seven-year main-line boiler ticket, No 4498 was withdrawn after the Shildon exhibition and did not reappear on the main line until April 1977. On 30 April she worked an A4 Locomotive Society special from York to the locomotive's new base at Carnforth. On the night before, the A4LS held a dinner alongside the locomotive in the NRM to celebrate the centenary of Sir Nigel's birth. A six-year period of operation now followed, which included an appearance at the 'Rocket 150' cavalcade at Rainhill on 24-26 May 1980. In the autumn of 1982, No 4498 was again withdrawn for overhaul, including re-tubing. This took until 9 June 1984, when No 4498

October 1967 found No 4498 on the West Coast Main Line heading an SLS special between Crewe and Carlisle. On 28 October the locomotive tears through Tebay and attacks the 1 in 75 climb to Shap with the 11-coach train.
T. G. Hepburn/IAL

made a triumphant return to the main line with a private charter from Clitheroe to York via Manchester and Leeds. The locomotive now ran for a further six years, including a special programme of four trains in 1987 to celebrate her 50th birthday and the 21st anniversary of its ownership by the A4 Locomotive Society. On 27 March 1989, No 4498 suffered a bent left eccentric rod at High Wycombe while working the return 'Peaks Express' from Marylebone to Derby. In late June, during a routine examination at Didcot, serious cracking was discovered round the throat plate washout plug. The A4LS

After enforced idleness between 1968 and 1972, No 4498 worked in that and the following year, then on 22 June 1974 worked the 'Tyne-Dee Coastal' special from Edinburgh to Aberdeen and back. The gleaming 'A4' gets into her stride through Princes Street Gardens on leaving Edinburgh, bound for Aberdeen. *Millar/IAL*

made the difficult decision to bring forward by two years the seven-year overhaul, and the locomotive was towed to Carnforth on 17 July 1989.

This third overhaul in preservation took until 1992, with the test run round the Derby circuit being undertaken on 27 August. The planned return to service on 30 August was frustrated by a cracked bogie axlebox horn cheek detected after the 27th run and a derailment at Carnforth on 5 September, immediately before working a Farington to Carlisle 'Gold and Silver Jubilee' special to celebrate the 25th anniversary of A4LS ownership of the locomotive and the 50th anniversary of Ian Allan Publishing Ltd. After a brief visit to the Severn Valley Railway, No 4498 finally returned to the main line at the head of a 'Cumbrian Mountain Limited' from Bradford Forster Square to Carlisle on 21 November 1992. This time No 4498 managed to achieve the full seven-year operation, running until 1999. Following an intermediate overhaul in 1995 the A4LS held a poll of members that resulted in a change of identity for No 4498. This was back to No 60007 and the BR dark blue with black-and-white lining, which the locomotive carried from September 1950 to April 1952. A highlight of this period of

Prior to featuring in the 'Rocket 150' celebrations at Rainhill, No 4498 was stabled with three other locomotives in the still-active locomotive shed at Northwich, where I was BR Area Manager. Owing to pressure for access to the locomotives at a working shed, I decided to hold an 'Open Day' on Sunday 18 May 1980. *Sir Nigel Gresley* and No 35028 *Clan Line* were used in 'top-and-tail' mode between two coaches to provide passenger shuttles, with Nos 80079 and 5000 as alternatives. As No 4498 departs with the shuttle, 2-6-4T No 80079 can be seen in the background outside the shed. *P. Groom*

On 9 June 1984,
No 4498 *Sir Nigel Gresley* blackens the sky over Leeds as she departs for Manchester and Clitheroe past Whitehall Junction with a return 'Clitheronian' private charter from York.
Peter Skelton/IAL

In the winter of 1985 snow lay on the ground well into February. On 26 January No 4498 had headed the inaugural 'Thames-Avon Express', which had become an instant success, and here the returning fourth train on 16 February climbs the gradient through the snow-covered landscape between Stratford-upon-Avon and Wilmcote.
J. H. Cooper-Smith/IAL

In a classic pose on 30 August 1984, No 4498 roars over the River Ribble at Sheriff's Brow, climbing the 15-mile-long 1 in 100 'long drag' to Blea Moor with the northbound 'Cumbrian Mountain Pullman'.
Brian Dobbs/IAL

operation was the 1995 'Shap Time Trials' over 30 September and 2/3 October, when successive trains were operated from Crewe to Carlisle via Shap, returning via the S&C and Blackburn. No 60007 worked the first run on 30 September, with subsequent days being operated by No 71000 *Duke of Gloucester* and No 46229 *Duchess of Hamilton*. After working a King's Cross-Scarborough-York special on 16 June 1999, No 60007 was worked to the North Yorkshire Moors Railway, which had become the locomotive's new home base and the location for the fourth overhaul.

This overhaul became the locomotive's most comprehensive (and expensive!) since preservation in 1967. In addition to the usual items it included the installation of an air-braking control system and both the TPWS and Data Recording systems that have now become a requirement for operation on the main line. Fortunately, the support of the Heritage Lottery Fund was obtained and the locomotive returned to traffic with an NYMR special train for Sir Nigel Gresley Locomotive Preservation Trust members on 31 March 2007. The new and onerous bureaucracy that is a requirement for main-line operation proved slow and tortuous, and the 'Derogation from Group Standards' obligatory for a main-line 'ticket' was not finally obtained until 28 February 2008. Over the 40 years that No 4498/60007 has been in private ownership the locomotive has

A classic panning shot shows the full grace and elegance of an 'A4' as *Sir Nigel Gresley* passes Kettlebeck with the northbound 'Cumbrian Mountain Pullman' on 24 August 1985. *Alan Barnes/IAL*

Not the East Coast Main Line in the 1960s, but No 4498 *Sir Nigel Gresley* piloting 'Deltic' No 55015 *Tulyar* through Saunderton on 14 June 1986 with a High Wycombe to Aylesbury empty stock train for an Aylesbury Open Day. *Mick Alderman/IAL*

A highlight of 1986 was the series of 15 'Blackmore Vale Express' trains between Salisbury and Yeovil. The last train ran on Sunday 26 October and is seen here with No 4498 climbing steadily towards Buckhorn Weston Tunnel with the outward trip. *Mark S. Wilkins/IAL*

operated on the main line for 24 years, the remainder being accounted for by the four general overhauls that have been undertaken. Who would have thought in 1966 that 42 years later, in the year 2008, we would be able to experience main-line workings by all three operational 'A4s', Nos 60007 *Sir Nigel Gresley*, 60009 *Union of South Africa* and 60019 *Bittern*, a feat only achieved twice since 1966, in 1973 and 1986!

No 4488/60009 *Osprey/Union of South Africa*

The fifth 'A4' to be preserved, No 60009 *Union of South Africa*, was always a Scottish-based locomotive and was withdrawn from Ferryhill shed on 1 June 1966. A group of four Scottish business associates led by John Cameron acquired the locomotive in July 1966 and, after several months in storage at Ferryhill, it was moved to Thornton in Fife. While there it acquired a 62A Thornton shed plate. No 60009 had one last blaze of glory on 25 March 1967 when it was used to haul a Scottish Region railtour between Perth and Aberdeen and between Stirling and Edinburgh, after which the locomotive returned light to Thornton shed. On 8 April 1967 it was moved by rail to Crail and thence by road to the specially constructed 3-mile-long Lochty Private Railway near Anstruther in Fife, where it made its first run on 14 June 1967.

With the return to steam in 1972, No 60009 was not initially listed as a suitable locomotive for inclusion in the 'pool', presumably because of her land-locked location. The urge to return to the main line proved irresistible, however, and 'No 9' made the first Scottish return-to-steam trip on 5 May 1973 with the first of three dates for a return trip from Inverkeithing to Dundee. Subsequent Scottish trips followed in 1974 and 1975, 1978/79/80 and 1983. The return to working south of the border was eventually achieved in 1984 when 'No 9' participated in a series of Settle & Carlisle and 'Scarborough Spa' services. In 1985 a move to London was frustrated when a broken spring at York on 25 May caused cancellation of the move south, and 'No 9' returned

By April 1984 'No 9' has moved south of the border for the first time since preservation in 1967, and here approaches Shotlock Hill with a northbound 'Cumbrian Mountain Express' on 20 April. Later in the journey she was blamed for a severe lineside fire north of Appleby, which caused the trip a week later to be hauled by D200 from Appleby to Carlisle.
J. H. Cooper-Smith/IAL

No 60009 *Union of South Africa* returned to the main line in 1973, and ten years later, on the occasion of the Ayr Railfair on 29/30 October 1983, she was used to work a special train from Edinburgh to Ayr outwards on the Saturday, returning on the Sunday. Here 'No 9' approaches Paisley *en route* to Ayr on the Saturday outward working.
Colin Boocock/IAL

In 1985 the plan was that 'No 9' would work south to Marylebone to share in 'Shakespeare Express' workings, but a broken driving wheel spring sidelined the locomotive for more than two months at York, which was as far south as she managed. Here, after repairs, she heads the southbound 'Cumbrian Mountain Express' just short of Ais Gill summit on 14 September.
J. H. Cooper-Smith/IAL

The Centenary of the Forth Bridge was celebrated on 4 March 1990, and what more appropriate locomotive to work the special trains than 'No 9', fresh off a general overhaul at Bridgnorth Works? As she found herself the potential target of anti-apartheid protests, a reversion to her original *Osprey* name was felt appropriate. After working the VIP special in the morning 'No 9' worked an afternoon 'The Forth Centennial' public special from Edinburgh to Perth and back. Here the train gets away from Haymarket on the outward journey to Perth.
W. A. Sharman/IAL

In the summer of 1990 BR sponsored a series of 'North Wales Coast Express' services running on three days each week from Crewe to Holyhead. On 22 August 'No 9' is pictured at speed between Conwy and Penmaenmawr with the outward service.
John B. Gosling/IAL

On 19 September 1991, No 60009 was rededicated as *Union of South Africa* in a ceremony at Waverley station, then worked a special for the VIP guests to Dundee via Stirling and Perth. Here she heads north from Stirling with the 'raspberry ripple' 1st Class dining set.
T. J. Gregg/IAL

north on 30 November with a York to Carlisle train via Leeds and Settle. In 1986 No 60009 worked a Perth-Edinburgh-Perth-Dundee train on 5 July, in connection with the Commonwealth Games then taking place in Edinburgh. The need for a general overhaul saw the locomotive move south to the Severn Valley Railway, which was to become its new home base for the next 11 years until 1997.

1990 was the centenary year of the Forth Bridge and 'No 9' was earmarked for a series of special trains on 4 March. With the turmoil at the end of the apartheid regime in South Africa it was thought that *Union of South Africa* could attract anti-apartheid demonstrators, which would detract from the celebrations, so the locomotive temporarily reverted to her original name *Osprey*. The overhaul was a close-run thing, with the successful test run being completed on 22 February before a 24 February run without nameplates from Carlisle to Skipton, after which the locomotive retired to Carnforth for more adjustments before heading to Edinburgh for the 4 March Forth Bridge trips. 'No 9' was then used by BR for a month of crew training trips round Fife. Later in the year No 60009 worked a number of both 'Cumbrian Mountain Express' and 'North Wales Coast Express' services. Continuing regular employment in England, Wales and Scotland followed in 1991, with 'No 9' disguised as No 60004 *William Whitelaw* to work a special between Edinburgh and Glasgow Queen Street on 16 February in order to celebrate 150 years of the NBR Edinburgh and Glasgow route. A further period of repairs followed before a return to the main line on 8 June 1993 with a Scotrail-chartered Perth to Glasgow special. Intended to operate five days a week for a month, this was terminated on the first day when a failed steam joint in the cab caused the Traction Inspector to be severely scalded. The programme was reinstated and ran successfully in October. In 1994 the highlight was on 29 and 30 October when 'No 9' worked the first steam trains out of King's Cross for 25 years to Peterborough and return. In 1995 she worked from Waterloo to Southampton on 22 January and to Exeter on 18 February, returning to Paddington on the 19th. 'No 9' worked extensively throughout the rest of 1995 and 1996 before retiring to the SVR for yet another overhaul after a 5 October Peterborough to York and return trip.

No 60009 reappeared on the main line in 2002 and operated extensively throughout 2002-06 and 2007. Early in the latter year John Cameron announced that

he had acquired the former diesel shed at Thornton from EWS as a home for his two main-line locomotives, 'No 9' and No 61994 *The Great Marquess*, and intended to relocate the 'A4' from the Severn Valley Railway to her original 1966 home at Thornton as soon as this was ready. The locomotive's seven-year boiler ticket expires in 2008, but this would still allow the simultaneous operation on the main line of three 'A4s' for most of that year.

No 4464/60019 *Bittern*

Just a week after the withdrawal of the last operational 'A4s' on 5 September 1966, one of them, No 60019 *Bittern*, was bought by a consortium headed by Geoff Drury of York. Mr Drury had already made arrangements for 'No 19' to be housed in the LNER North

A week after withdrawal by BR in September 1966, No 60019 *Bittern* was sold to Geoff Drury and became the sixth and final 'A4' to be saved. Arrangements had already been made to stable the locomotive in the north roundhouse at York shed – today's Great Hall of the National Railway Museum. After moving south from Aberdeen No 60019 was steamed by BR for one last occasion prior to handover and was used to haul a Class 8 freight between Skelton yard at York and Healey Mills yard, west of Wakefield. Here the 'A4', still claiming to belong to Ferryhill shed, departs from Skelton for Healey Mills with her last BR working. *IAL*

During 1967, No 60019 *Bittern* was used on a number of specials, and here on 16 July she heads north through Newlay & Horsforth with a Leeds to Carlisle RCTS special.
Alan Bailey/IAL

A brace of 'A4s' have an unusual companion. Even before the advent of the NRM, York shed was used to stable visiting steam locomotives, and here, in August 1967, No 60019's temporary home in the roundhouse is shared by, on the left, No 4498 *Sir Nigel Gresley*, and on the right No 7029 *Clun Castle*.
Rodney Wildsmith/IAL

On 4 November 1967 *Bittern* hurries along above the North Sea coast near Burnmouth as she works an RCTS Leeds to Edinburgh excursion. This was No 60019's last working before the infamous BR ban on main-line steam was implemented, not rescinded until 1972. After a handful of runs in 1972 and 1973 No 60019 then retired from the main line and had to wait until 2007 before reappearing.
Paul Claxton/IAL

roundhouse at York shed, today's Great Hall of the National Railway Museum. After moving south from Aberdeen to York some adjustments were made that required a test run, so arrangements were made for 'No 19' to work a freight train from Skelton yard at York to Healey Mills and back. After this the loco emerged from York on several occasions to work main-line specials including a couple for the RCTS from Leeds to Scotland, the last of which ran on 4 November 1967. With the closure of York shed, No 60019 was moved to Neville Hill at Leeds for several years before a spell at Dinting.

With the return to steam in 1972 *Bittern* appeared on the 'approved' list and worked several services including, on 16 September 1972, a 'Scarborough Flyer' from York to Scarborough and Hull. Two trips were worked in 1973: on 22 April 'No 19' relieved No 4498 *Sir Nigel Gresley* at Scarborough for a trip to Hull, then on 17 June from York to Scarborough and back. The very small group of helpers assisting Mr Drury were unable to maintain the locomotive, so 'No 19' began a long period of inactivity. For the 50th anniversary, in 1988, of *Mallard*'s World Record the NELPG offered to cosmetically restore the rather neglected and forlorn 'No 19' and a deal was negotiated with Geoff Drury for them to be custodians of the locomotive.

An imaginative idea was enthusiastically taken up when the locomotive was cosmetically restored, not as No 4464 but with a single chimney restored and in silver-and-grey livery as No 2509 *Silver Link*. The NELPG already had huge restoration commitments with Peppercorn Pacific No 532 *Blue Peter*, so no work was done on 'No 19' after the *Silver Link* identity change.

After the death of Geoff Drury his family sold the locomotive to businessman Jeremy Hosking and the new owner arranged for movement from Teesside to the Mid Hants Railway at Ropley, where the contract restoration to full main-line working order began in 2005. Restored to late BR condition as No 60019 *Bittern*, the first steamings took place in June 2007, with a first main-line passenger run performed on 1 December from King's Cross to York, returning to Finsbury Park on 15 December.

So in 2008 there were three main-line-certificated 'A4s' for the first time since 1986, with all the opportunities that brought to enjoy the unique sound and fury of some of the best-loved products of one of the UK's most charismatic locomotive designers. Saturday 5 July 2008 should be a very special day at York as it is planned that all three operational 'A4s' will be there together with No 4468 *Mallard*.

Not what it seems: in 1988, as part of the celebrations of the 50th anniversary of *Mallard*'s record run, NELPG, then the custodians of No 60019 *Bittern*, arranged for a cosmetic restoration of the unserviceable locomotive as the long-lost original 'A4' No 2509 *Silver Link*. This involved replacement of the double chimney she had carried since 1957 with an original-style single chimney and restoration of the side-skirting, removed during wartime. Restoration of the original recessed front coupling and short buffers, which in any case No 2509 only carried for her first ten months in service, was not considered worthwhile for this one-off exercise.
Maurice Burns/IAL

As part of the anniversary celebrations, a special line-up of 'A4s' was arranged outside the National Railway Museum at York. Here, in July 1988, from right to left, are, first, in LNER Garter blue livery with stainless steel cut-out numbers and letters, No 4498 *Sir Nigel Gresley*; then, in LNER silver-and-grey 'Silver Jubilee' livery is the repainted No 60019 *Bittern*, masquerading as long-scrapped *Silver Link*; then, in LNER Garter blue with the full streamlined skirting, No 4468 *Mallard* as preserved in the NRM. *National Railway Museum/Colour-Rail P233*

'A4 escape': No 60008 *Dwight D. Eisenhower* rests in preservation at Green Bay, Wisconsin, USA, in November 1985. The locomotive is posed at the head of four UK passenger carriages, including the Pullman car 'Lydia', and stands in front of former Union Pacific 'Big Boy' No 4017. After cosmetic restoration at Doncaster in July 1963 the locomotive was shipped from Southampton to the USA on 27 April 1964 and has subsequently been repainted in an incorrect shade of Brunswick green. Currently presenting a rather neglected and unloved appearance, there have been calls for the former No 4496 *Golden Shuttle* to be repatriated. *Bill Reagles/IAL*

No 60009 *Union of South Africa* has undergone several identity changes in preservation. First, for the Forth Bridge centenary services in 1990; and to avoid threatened 'anti-apartheid' demonstrations, she re-acquired her original *Osprey* name. After an overhaul in 1991 she operated initially as No 60027 *Merlin* and is seen here on 31 August of that year on her trial run preparing to attack the 1 in 82 gradient of Gresford bank between Chester and Wrexham. The actual No 60027 (ex-No 4486) had been broken up by G. H. Campbell at Sheildhall in December 1965. *N. Wellings/IAL*

In 1990 the Forth Bridge celebrated its centenary and No 60009 was used to work a number of celebratory runs. Having reverted to her original name, in this view from March 1990, No 60009 *Osprey* poses on the turntable at Perth, having arrived with a Forth Bridge special from Edinburgh. *Colour-Rail P320*